The Hijacked Brain

The Hijacked Brain

Overcoming Internal Barriers
To a Happily Ever After

Nathalie Concepcion, MSW, LCSW
and
Bob McCullough, Ph.D, LCSW

AMARNA
BOOKS & MEDIA

www.amarnabooksandmedia.com

The Hijacked Brain

Published by Amarna Books & Media, Maplewood, New Jersey

This publication contains the opinions and ideas of the authors. It is intended to provide helpful and informative material on the subject matter covered. It is sold with the understanding that the authors and publisher are not engaged in rendering professional services in the book. If the reader requires personal assistance or advice, a competent professional should be consulted. The authors and publisher specifically disclaim any responsibility for any liability, loss, or risk, personal or otherwise, which is incurred as a consequence, directly or indirectly, of the use and application of any of the contents of this book. No liability is assumed for damages resulting from the use of information contained within.

ISBN-10: 0-9828951-5-1
ISBN-13: 978-0-9828951-5-3

Book and cover design by Thomas Edward West of Amarna Books and Media
Cover photograph: Konrad Bak, Adobe Stock

Contents

Acknowledgments

Nathalie's Acknowledgments

A deep token of appreciation to the many couples that have placed their trust in me to create the best version of their relationship.

Deeper token to my ex-husband Charles, for supporting my love of learning for 25 years and inspiring my interest in couples' success.

And deepest token of appreciation yet to Bob, my co-writer and dear friend, for asking the questions and helping me believe the answers were worth writing.

Nathalie's Dedication

To my children, Chelsea, Charlie and Christopher; may my spoken and written words stay with you and help you in the pursuit to be whole people no matter what you go through. And may my words also help you to never contribute to anyone's undoing.

Read on... which is to say: Onward!

Bob's Acknowledgments

This book is about relationships and therefore I want to acknowledge the most important relationships I have. My wonderful wife Angela whose crazy matches my crazy and has been very supportive when I decide to try something new.

My children Cam, Nick and Emily. Those of you who have kids know what an incredible blessing and gift they are when they are young, impressionable and full of unlimited energy. However, they are now adults and it amazes me everyday to see how blessed I am at the individuals they have become. They love, laugh, work hard, love God and love their mom...which is exactly what I could have hoped.

I also need to thank greatly Nathalie for entertaining the idea of starting this project. She has so much insight, knowledge and love for all that everyone who reads this book, listens to an interview with her or has a chance just to talk with her will walk away feeling inspired, motivated, energized and ready to take on anything.

Bob's Dedication

Love. Its what guides us, motivates us and completes us. When you know true love there will be peace, joy, kindness, goodness, patience, faithfulness, gentleness and self-control. All the components that you need to have a happy, successful relationship. Seek love above all else and you will have everything you ever needed.

Setting the Stage

One of the tools we will use to illustrate the way a Hijacked Brain influences relationships are stories from real couples. The stories come from people who have sought our therapeutic assistance; the names have been changed and some of the couples are composites of different couples to further protect identities. Here are three of the couples you will meet:

Couple #1

**Trevor
& Alyssa**

Couple #1, Trevor and Alyssa, were married for 7 years after a two-year courtship. They met right after college and quickly developed an exclusive romantic relationship, during which they realized they had many things in common, including career goals, social interests, and mutual friends. Alyssa is a trainer for a pharmaceutical company and travels often, sometimes for two weeks at a time. Trevor works for a small information technology firm as a software developer, but rarely travels for his work.

While dating, they found common interests such as restaurants and njoying the local scene, including music festivals and getting together with friends. However, after seven years of marriage, they have settled into a routine that has moved away from the activities they used to share as a couple. Alyssa enjoys reading and is often engaged in a book when at home or on the weekends. Trevor is very focused on video games where he has developed an online network of friends. He will often spend hours in his "man-cave" playing games and interacting online.

They report that during their dating and courtship, communication was great. It was a time of exploration and curiosity, although Alyssa reported that even while dating she could see herself taking the responsibility to start conversations and keep them

moving forward. Trevor agreed to that statement, saying that he would gladly participate and not hinder conversations but did not initiate them. He admitted he would share thoughts on topics but never got emotionally invested in their conversations. Alyssa admitted she always wanted more from Trevor, but convinced herself that relationships take time and that their relationship would continue to grow through the years.

Trevor reports that he enjoyed his time with Alyssa while they were dating. He was very attracted to her physically, liked that she was driven in her career and was pleasant to be around. He admitted he had not dated until he met her. Trevor had always been more interested in his "gaming," but after graduating from college and securing a "real" job, he was feeling the pressure to meet someone and be married. Alyssa had what he was seeking in a mate, and while he thought that initially she asked too many questions, he was interested enough to keep moving forward in the relationship, thinking that's just "how she is."

They sought counseling for a few different reasons: the first is that they both agree that their communication and interaction had changed over the past several years. They do not know when, why, or how it started, but they realize neither is happy with the current trend. Second is that Trevor has struggled with understanding his wife's expressions of love. Alyssa does not always verbalize that she loves him. Instead, she expects that Trevor knows because she is with him and does things with him. Third, he was unfaithful to her. They both want to stay in the marriage.

Couple #2

Annie & Jamie

Annie and Jamie have a unique history together. They have known each other for a very long time, growing up in the same neighborhood and going to school together. They began dating during their senior year of high school and moved in together the following year. While living together, both attended schools; Annie became a dental hygienist and Jamie an electrician. After living together for a few years, they married and began a family with the birth of their daughter, 4, and son, 2.

Initially, their relationship was very enmeshed. Annie found it very difficult to experience any positive emotions when they were apart. She was clear that she did not like to be alone. When she started dating Jamie, she wanted to spend every moment with him and found herself thinking only about him when they were apart. Jamie initially enjoyed the attention, especially the physical part of the relationship, which began early in their dating. After a period of time, Jamie began to feel smothered and spoke with Annie regarding their need to have other interests. At first, Annie saw this as rejection by Jamie, but was committed to trying to please him and provide what he needed.

Recently, their communication has been marked by reactions instead of understanding and support. Annie has been less willing to control her outbursts and Jamie has been more explosive. All areas of their life have been impacted, as they do not enjoy family time, they have disagreements on raising the children, and their sexual intimacy has stopped. They have come to counseling because both would like to see a change in how they communicate. They both fear that they are walking down a path towards divorce if their current interactions are not improved.

Couple #3

Janet
& Ricky

Ricky and Janet have been married for 20 years. Friends and family thought they had the perfect, great marriage. With two children, one in college and the other finishing high school this year, many thought they were entering the time of their marriage where they would be free to be a couple again, but they were plagued by unresolved issues.

First was their children, Michael and Christine. The kids were great. They were good in sports and very active in multiple activities which required the "divide and conquer" approach. Ricky would take one to practice while Janet had the other. The practices and away game schedules seldom coincided, so while the kids always knew that one parent would be there, rarely were both Ricky and Janet together for a game. They lost their individual identity to become Michael's mom or Christine's dad and, with that, they also began to lose their grip on their marriage. As the kids started to become more independent, Ricky and Janet struggled to know how or where they fit.

The next factor was careers. Janet had become a very successful Human Resource manager and found a great deal of satisfaction in the status and responsibility she had in the office. She had built her career on the ability to communicate and help others grow into their potential. Work was a very positive experience for her as she felt important and needed.

Ricky had struggled recently in his career. As a general contractor, the unstable economy often made a "feast or famine" situation with his work. When times were good, he was very busy and enjoyed being able to provide for his family. But when work was not available he struggled with thoughts of not being "good enough". He was concerned he was not living up to Janet's needs and expectations, even though he had never asked her what those were and she had never made negative comments about the instability of his work.

The final factor that played a role in their relationship was family history. While Janet's parents were still married after 48 years, Ricky's parents had divorced when he was a teenager. He had witnessed—and was the product of—dysfunctional family life. Janet always admired her parents' marriage and relationship, and hoped that hers would be modeled after theirs. Ricky hoped and planned that he would do everything different from his parents' marriage.

Go ahead!
Write in
the book!

Reader's Thoughts

Do any of these scenarios look or feel like yours?

How would you describe your current situation?

Have you considered how your current situation got started?

If we were meeting today, how would you characterize your relationship and your role in it?

The Hijacked Brain

chapter one

What is a "Hijacked Brain"?

Defining the title of this book requires some explanation. Early on in our many years working with couples seeking to improve their relationships, a pattern started to emerge. The couples would report peaks and valleys in their relationships. The peaks would be described as days of seeming synergy when both partners felt at ease, safe, and satisfied in and with the relationship. The valleys would be characterized by an inability to connect with any efforts to do so, igniting arguments.

After some investigation, many couples—in fact, too many not to notice—would mention some ability to determine when the valleys would begin. The Hijacked Brain is code for the emotional and behavioral experience for both men and women during those spaces of time.

The Hijacked Brain is defined as a period of time (moments, hours or days) when an individual feels carried away by emotions and is unable to feel in control of reactions and thoughts. While this experience can run the gamut from mild to severe, all who are affected report disruptions in the management of life, with clear consequences to their most precious relationships.

It would be simple if we could postulate that women were the only ones reporting a Hijacked Brain, as it is common for women to be emotionally affected by their menstrual cycle. But the reality is that men, too, are exposed to experiencing this phenomenon. Some causes affecting men and women include anniversaries of losses, trauma, or emotional hurt; being overextended, stressed, or overly tired; manic or depressed stages, or bipolar disorder or other diagnosable behaviors or internal experiences.

People describe the Hijacked Brain as a gamut of negative experiences that include feeling overwhelmed, irrational, rapid or uncontrollable negative thinking, inability to manage emotions, heightened sensitivity, difficulty expressing thoughts, anxiety, bouts of depression, increased fault-finding in people around them (in and out of their romantic relationships), and difficulty feeling in control of their behavior.

Reader's Thoughts

Do you notice when your brain is hijacked?

We all have default behaviors when in Hijacked Brain mode. Can you list a few of yours?

Can you identify the way that your default behaviors affect your partner?

chapter two

Why was this book written?

Our interest in writing the book stemmed from observing the similarities in the challenges and potential solutions as well as the foreseeable benefit to so many. Too many people are in pain and their pain is going on without acknowledgement, without recognizing the common nature of their experiences, and with little understood about the many options available to help rise above. The issues and situations caused by this syndrome have been the basis of jokes and used as excuses for questionable behavior. The Hijacked Brain has also been cited as a reason for self-limiting beliefs and, as alluded to above, very frequently kept as a secret that too many are afraid of or unwilling to talk about.

Our intention is to give voice to the experience of millions of men and women affected by Hijacked Brains, and to expose possible causes and potential solutions in an effort to limit or eliminate emotional and psychological pain.

Our approach will be holistic and will offer tools that include physical, emotional, spiritual, and psychological perspectives on this topic.

Additionally, we have been mindful of the professionals who may reach for this book in order to help patients and clients. You, too, will find a wealth of information, including a web portal that connects you to additional resources, frequently asked questions, how to reach the authors, trainings, and more. *www.fireintheweeds.com*

By holistic approach we mean interventions that address the individual as a whole and tether within and outside conventional medical and clinical thought.

We have made every effort to create a valuable tool with practical uses for all readers.

Who is this book written for?

This book is for individuals and couples who are questioning if there is a way to experience less suffering as they support each other and manage their own Hijacked Brains. It is for those invested in their personal growth and committed to improving the valuable relationships in their lives.

While directed toward couples, we believe that the new understanding provided in these pages, coupled with the skills and strategies discussed, can help any reader improve all relationships.

If there was one prerequisite to take full advantage of the principles we share, that prerequisite would be that the reader must focus on his or her own experience and avoid using this information to blame, justify, or find fault in others. We acknowledge the many ways mood changes inflict pain and create challenges in the everyday lives of individuals, couples, families, and other types of relationships. There are pearls of wisdom for people in all categories.

Our goal is to provide a wealth of information that will improve all relationships.

What will the reader learn or gain?

The reader will learn the basic reasons that may cause a Hijacked Brain and the potential long-term and short-term consequences of that phenomenon. We will pay close attention to how these changes affect an individual's self-esteem, view of self, and their direct impact in relationships. Additionally, we will give voice to the emotional experience for those sharing the relationship, including the ways in which their involvement impacts their own self-esteem, view of self, and their impact on the relationship in question.

After laying a firm foundation of understanding, we will look at common dynamics and discuss skills and strategies that facilitate communication, collaboration, and partnership with the ultimate goal of reducing emotional pain for all involved. The gains will include:

- Heightened self-awareness
- Improved emotional intelligence
- Ability to thrive during emotionally difficult times
- Increased personal accountability
- Lifting of mood, increase in hope
- Specific strategies and coping mechanisms
- Purposeful behaviors proven to enhance the enjoyment of life

---

The Hijacked Brain was written both as a text and a workbook. It is meant for people who directly and indirectly feel the effects of a Hijacked Brain. It is for helping professionals and or anyone seeking to understand and possibly manage the challenges associated with this experience.

How does the book work?

The book is divided into easy-to-identify sections with chapters, tools, and thinking pages to enhance the learning experience. The reader is encouraged to read the foundational chapters first (*What is a "Hijacked Brain?*, *Why Was This Book Written?*, *The Science of a Hijacked Brain*) as we believe they hold the key to the development of understanding and compassion, which will lead the way of learning, changing, and growing for the individual and the relationship's benefit.

Our intention is to communicate in such a way that our message is understood clearly and without ambivalence.

It is beneficial to share the book with those who take part in the relationship in question. Mutual learning, open conversations about the topics covered, and strategizing as a team can have a great impact as well as nurture growth and transformation. If not possible, readers must concentrate on their personal learning and, as mentioned before, avoid using this information to find fault in others or justify behavior. Suggestions are given to those reading the book on their own in the chapter titled *Going It Alone*.

Lastly, we have made an effort to define words and phrases as we mean them (see definitions offered in text boxes throughout the book as well as in the chapter dedicated to this purpose). Our goal is to ensure that the writers and the readers adhere to specific meanings and avoid misinterpretation.

As mentioned above, the book is sprinkled with tools and thinking pages. These are intended for your use. The more honest and open you allow yourself to be, the more effective the book. That is to say, the deeper you go into the work, the greater the possibility for personal improvement.

Make your experience more meaningful by logging onto our website *www.fireintheweeds.com* for new content, join our discussion on Facebook, follow us on Twitter, or find a clinician who utilizes these tools to help individuals and couples. We are committed to supporting your learning and assisting in the improvement and longevity of your relationship.

For your convenience, we have included a resource section which is a compilation of recommended websites, authors, treatments, and strategies.

Reader's Thoughts

What points mentioned seem to be of special interest to you?

chapter three

The Science of a Hijacked Brain

In order to fully understand how a Hijacked Brain functions and how it impacts our intimate relationships, it is important to consider several of the more frequent causes.

As we explore potential causes, please know that:

1. We are all exposed to potential causes at some point, but to different degrees;
2. Some of the causes listed are unique to genders, but impact all involved;

3. These causes are not presented to indicate blame;
4. Having the ability to see how the issues presented affect us individually will bear more fruit than assigning the offered labels to others.

We strongly acknowledge that mental health,
developmental, and personal history issues, as well as
personality disorders and even culturally-driven beliefs
help us to gain insight into what causes the Hijacked
Brain, but in no way place fault on the individual for the
clinical issues that affect them. To take this further, our
discussion places responsibility for behavior—but not
blame—for the causation of issues.

Trevor

Trevor was experiencing frequent mood swings which caused his spouse to report a feeling of "walking on eggshells." They had done clinical work to repair the relationship, but noticed they continued to be affected by the swings (Hijacked Brain). In looking for organic reasons, it was documented that Trevor was only sleeping 4 to 5 hours per night, often non-consecutively. A sleep study was completed and recommendations were followed. Once settled into the new sleep routine, the couple reported a decrease in mood swings as well as greater ability to argue productively when needed.

Lack of Sleep

Sleep is a basic need and critically affects how we function. Too often, sleep is considered a luxury, but it is imperative to support wellness, manage emotions, and control behavior. Our brain needs sleep in order to recover from trauma (be it physical, psychological, or emotional), strengthen its ability to process information, store memories, and promote creative ways of thinking, among many other functions. Sleep deprivation has been linked to increased physical illness such as elevated blood pressure, diabetes, and heart disease.

Additionally, lack of sleep can impact our mental health and cause irritability, bouts of anger, depression, and even dementia over time. Lack of sleep impacts our ability to handle stress. Research has shown that an individual requires no less than five hours of consecutive sleep in order for the brain to manage and accomplish all its functions properly. Sleep hygiene should be discussed with health providers on a regular basis and must be reviewed before assigning or accepting any diagnosis, as too often improved sleep patterns will resolve a host of physical and emotional issues.

Nutrition

So much is discussed about the harmful impact of a poor diet that many of us already perceive this topic as white noise. But nutrition can, in fact, have an impact on our behavior, mood, ability to manage stress, etc. It is well known that certain foods like saturated fats, sugars, and alcohol can negatively impact health and cause physical health issues like diabetes, heart disease, fatigue, obesity, and other issues.

Eating healthy meals and getting proper nutrition goes beyond improving energy levels and helping to ensure optimal brain function. When addressing behavioral concerns with a medical professional, discussing nutritional issues is a must. We have seen individuals diagnosed with depression when, in fact, the issue was a vitamin D deficiency. Because the impact of our nutritional habits can have such an impact, learning and applying gained insight to what we choose to eat will, to a great extent, help to determine overall well-being.

Additionally, we have found that outside of nutrition, eating on a schedule is something that many do not consider important. It is often that couples get into arguments because one or both parties focus intensely on tasks to be completed (the job, the kids, community responsibilities) and either forget or neglect to eat… so much so that by the time they stop to eat, they have already been irritable and unpleasant to their significant other and often to other people in their path. Regularly scheduled meals (even small ones) go a long way in the effort to manage mood and behavior.

When an individual does not manage his or her nutrition, the consequences go beyond weight. Picture an individual with type 2 diabetes. The original physical issue (obesity) is now complicated by a diagnosis of diabetes. The person reports severe sexual dysfunction. How is this person feeling in his or her intimate relationship?

When we are not taking good care of ourselves and feel the consequences of our personal neglect, those consequences go beyond weight at this point; anxiety, sadness, depression, lethargy—not to mention low self-esteem and poor behavior—start to creep into all areas of our lives.

Lack Of or Little Exercise

Like the behaviors mentioned above, exercise is important for brain chemistry balance. It helps our brain release endorphins while assisting the natural detoxifying process of the body. This in turn helps reduce stress, anxiety and depression. It improves mood, memory and concentration. It increases self-esteem and sense of well-being.

A sedentary life can cause a Hijacked Brain because the brain is not being provided with the oxygenation needed to be at its best and access the more powerful, higher-functioning areas in it.

Benny reported feeling depressed and could have been given a diagnosis of Clinical Depression. Upon assessment of his everyday routine, increased physical movement was recommended. He checked in with his primary care physician and chose an exercise routine that fit his schedule. Two weeks after getting started, he reported an improved mood. Three months later, he reported that he was no longer experiencing depressive symptoms. When asked what made him follow through with his regimen, he responded: "I feel healthy. The difference in my mood and self-esteem is exponential—I find myself wanting to do things and doing them confidently. That's what keeps me exercising."

Physical Illness

There are many types of physical illnesses and they all impact our brain and emotions. Cancer, heart disease, high blood pressure, hyper/hypothyroid, head injury, appendicitis, the flu… all have an impact on how the brain functions and, in turn, in how we process information, respond to everyday stressors, and how we behave towards our intimate partner and others. When the stressors of a physical illness hijack our brain, we feel tired, hopeless and helpless, not to mention that we are unable to behave in desirable ways.

Along with physical illness comes the difficulties associated with treatments prescribed to manage those illnesses. When Diana was diagnosed with breast cancer, chemotherapy caused irritability. Just when she was most in need of expressions of love, her mood made her behave in ways that pushed people away—including her strongest partner in the fight for her health: her husband.

Taking the effects of physical illness for granted will leave us exposed to reacting externally to our uncomfortable, often painful internal struggle. While taking care of our bodies is a priority, being mindful of our emotional, psychological, spiritual, and intellectual needs must take top position in our list of priorities. We are not just physical beings, and all our parts require attention, especially during a physical crisis.

Mental Illness

John

John has experienced depression for much of his adult life. The emotional pain has become unbearable enough for him to consider and attempt suicide. His wife recently stated, "if this happens again, I am out and I am taking our son with me." It is easy to see that while John's wife is not depressed, the impact of his illness is high. Furthermore, it has an intense impact on the relationship. The cascade of issues aggravates John's depression further. Nobody feels better or can figure out how to support the other. Left unattended, mental health will challenge good relationships and even destroy them.

The most often-asked question by spouses of people with mental illness is: "How do I get them to seek help?" The answer is too often rejected: "Look how you are enabling the unwanted behavior and stop doing that." Facing consequences of our behaviors is the most effective way to usher anyone to seek help. In too many cases, spouses and other close relatives and friends excuse behavior or rationalize it to such a degree that the identified patient does not recognize the impact they have in their own and others' lives.

Just as with physical illness, many of the medications and interventions used to treat mental illnesses can become an issue in relationships. Many psychotropic medications have side effects that may include lethargy, irritability, anxiety, and sexual dysfunction or disinterest, to name a few.

Couples going through treatment for a mental health diagnosis will greatly benefit from discussing the effects of treatment with a clinician who can assist the exponential improvement of communication, including open conversations of how to satisfy sexual needs while the treatment impedes the activities familiar to the individuals involved.

Personality Disorders

Personality disorders are diagnosable clinical issues that affect a person's view of the world, ability to interact/relate/communicate with others. Personality disorders can hijack a brain in terrible ways and cause great damage to relationships.

Carlos is an undiagnosed narcissist. He relates to the world as if it owed him something. His beliefs about his self-importance cause him to make quick decisions that affect personal and professional relationships. He is unable to seek professional help because he needs to feel in charge, and asking for assistance would move the scales away from his need for—and delusion of—control.

Carlos

Carol

Carol has been diagnosed with borderline personality disorder by three professionals. Regardless of those medical opinions, she sees herself as victimized and mistreated by most of the people in her life. Her most-used coping mechanism is triangulation, where she makes someone in her life "bad" in order to be able to relate to others. Drama and constant story-making complicate her life experience, and getting help is next to impossible, as she needs to feel that she is "right" and is not able to listen to or internalize feedback.

These examples do not encompass all that there is to be said about personality disorders, but they present a picture of the relationship challenges faced by people with personality disorders.

Age

Our age plays an important role in the makeup of our brain, thus our ability to manage behavior. Think back to our days as adolescents: the behavioral impact of changing hormones, as the brain developed and matured is undeniable. The same impact can be felt at other stages and the consequences are often the subject of jokes—the midlife crisis, grumpiness at old age, and other such examples come to mind.

Research in neuroplasticity informs us that, in fact, the brain is always changing, adapting, learning, maturing, and adjusting its response to new experiences. However, the appropriate development of our brain—especially when we are working to intentionally affect our outlook, mood, and behavior—requires purposeful care. Such care can take the form of therapy, meditation, medical care and follow-up as needed, physical exertion, rest, etc. These are all requirements to maintain healthy brain chemistry, but it is not an exhaustive list of all the things we can do to ensure personal wellness and relationship success as we age.

Susanne Schiebe found that our emotional experiences become more stable from one aging stage to the next, as well as more complex and calmer. But this is only true if we engage in persistent learning, willingly challenge limiting personal beliefs, and continuously dismiss any rigid ways of thinking. Leaving those unchallenged can create personal discomfort and relational friction.

Gender-Related Issues

Different cultures assign roles, responsibilities, and expectations to people given their gender. Regardless of the differences found from culture to culture, the pressures of those expectations can be daunting, and can cause individuals to lose their grip on behavior and produce relational issues.

Pedro

Pedro is 67 years old. His Hispanic background includes gender beliefs that insist that his self-esteem and lovability are attached to his ability to perform sexually. He lost his ability to have an erection five years ago after having prostate cancer. Today, he insists that his wife does not love him, despite outward evidence to the contrary.

Mary grew up in a strict religious system which insisted that women must constantly exercise charity and benevolence towards others and that women's specific purpose is to nurture others. She is overweight, tired, and constantly stressed out. She reports that she does not feel attractive and does not know how to relate to her husband outside of serving him. When asked what she does for her self-care, Mary responds, "I take care of myself by caring for others."

Mary

Arnold

Arnold grew up in a patriarchal society where men are in charge and must be responsible for the financial well-being of their family. He is a truck driver and works hard to provide for his family. He comes to therapy for anger management. After many sessions, it starts to become clear that his wife is financially successful and likes to make major decisions while he is away delivering a truckload. Arnold's anger stems from feelings of inadequacy and competition directly related to his culturally-developed gender beliefs.

While we cannot claim that cultural beliefs alter brain chemistry, we can postulate that rigid beliefs will challenge well-being and will critically influence behavior.

Trauma

The word *trauma* is a large umbrella that encompasses physical, psychological, and emotional hurts. Additionally, the severity of the trauma cannot be used to predetermine the severity of the reaction. In other words, when a number of people are exposed to the same trauma, each will recover at different speeds and levels. While some may be perceived as recovered, others will have consequences of the experience for a long time, if not for their whole life.

Trauma also has a way of being forgotten for a while and then springing up unexpectedly. The anniversary syndrome shows up often in treatment.

Marie

Marie reports that she is extremely sad and irritable. She is concerned that her mood is this dark despite the fact that all is well in her life: work is interesting and engaging, home is at peace and enjoyable. There is no visible cause to her discomfort. It took some stone-turning to realize that her mother had passed away five years ago, and while she had not felt this reaction before, this time she was expecting a child and had unwittingly been processing that her mother would not be part of the child's life.

Premenstrual Syndrome (PMS) and Premenstrual Dysphoric Disorder (PMDD)

For some women, the menstrual cycle is accompanied by uncomfortable physical symptoms, including pain—sometimes unbearable. Emotionally speaking, some women report that their cycle brings with it an upswing in mood.

chapter four

Going It Alone

Isolated, alone, lonely, secluded, desperate, fatigued, on your own, deserted, depressed, exhausted, tired, abandoned, rejected...these are some of the ways many of us feel in our intimate relationship.

First, we commend you for picking up this book and beginning to read. It indicates that you are interested in improving your relationship. We do realize, though, that many will be reading this alone—not necessarily by choice, but nonetheless reading, learning, and gaining insight that you wish your intimate partner was exposed to.

These next few pages are devoted to going a little deeper into what it means to "go it alone." You already know what this feels like, but we want you to know that your situation is not hopeless and you are not helpless.

Emotional abuse is often minimized, as it is difficult to prove and often relies on perception. Still, emotional abuse injures people and often takes them through cycles of desperation. Neglect, disregard, or denial of a partner's claims on relationships issues leave the individual questioning their sanity, and soon enough denying their intuition, assessments, and needs. For help identifying or treating emotional abuse, seek professional advice.

Feeling alone

Usually, individuals who are in committed, intimate relationships will define being alone as when they are physically separated from their intimate partner. However, others—too many—may feel alone all the time, even with their intimate partner close by. It may feel like one or more of the following:

Emotionally alone: There are many ways to describe being emotionally alone. Feeling "disconnected" even when in the same room. Feelings of rejection or, at a minimum, a lack of attention or interest prevail. Together and yet distant, with little to no motivation to address the issues that might improve the relationship; this, because there is no hope that the concerns will be given the same level of importance. There is no "emotional abuse" (or is there?) but the lack of interest to connect hurts. Longing for a partner to come along and experience every part of life feels overwhelmingly sad, not to mention frustrating as all you want is for them to see how different and satisfying life could be with just a little mindfulness and effort.

Physically alone: He is right there—and yet I am consumed with loneliness. Sound familiar? Consider these scenarios: Your intimate partner is a huge sports fan and is always watching a game. So he spends the night in the "man cave" with eyes glued on the TV, then the post-game and then SportsCenter that talks more about the game. Or, how about the intimate partner who is a big "gamer" and spends hours at a time on the computer, building empires or talking online with people around the world to "complete the mission." Better yet, sitting at dinner where instead of sharing about the day, life, each other—anything at all—everyone is on their phones, looking at what is happening in other people's lives.

Spiritually alone: Spirituality is not about religion, but about the priority given to being connected to a higher power. Too often, we look for life partners who share our religion, but not the placement they give to spiritual matters. Being spiritually alone is evident when we realize that our partner does not give this facet of life the same level of importance as we do. Rituals and spiritual activities are then individual endeavors; worse yet when our partners come along reluctantly, placing conditions on their attendance or do not feel touched or moved the same way we were, making comments that leave us wondering if we "made up" the experience.

Intellectually alone: Being intellectually alone is not about IQs but about what is important to bring up in conversation or passionate discussion. It's one partner enjoying talking about politics while the other wants to vomit at any discussion involving that topic. It is an inability to find a common interest in a topic; it's not that you don't agree, it's that the topic is not allowed. Because of this blockage, communication tends to be about a very limited range of topics. For the occasional acquaintance, this type of communication may be fine; for the intimate partner, the inability to have discussions about topics of interest can make anyone feel distant and alone.

Socially alone: Again, can you be together and yet separate? Do you have separate friend groups that do not cross or ever coexist? Do you really enjoy sports and being outside while your intimate partner prefers the opera and plays? Are you always sacrificing your needs and likes for your partner? Perhaps you are at the point of fatigue where you do not even want to try anymore because all you do is give. Give and take is expected—in fact, necessary for a healthy relationship, and required of both parties.

We are not designed to be alone. We are meant to share, love, laugh, and cry together. When you are trying to work on your relationship, make improvements, or address a desire, you need, want and yearn for your partner to be right there with you. This is an opportunity to work on all aspects of the relationship and bring your partner alongside to take an amazing journey together.

Reading the book on your own

Another alone activity! Here are some thoughts to improve the experience to reading on your own:

Read it for your benefit—too often our focus is so intent on fixing others that we miss opportunities to make ourselves better. Reading this book is meant to widen your perspective and provide support. By seeking personal growth, you can experience a transformation that may directly impact your most treasured relationship.

Use the information to understand instead of judge. Understanding others improves our ability to make ourselves understood.

Practice curiosity—just because we mention something does not make it so for your partner. Ask and listen. Use the principles taught in this book to include rather than deny the other's perspective.

We know that reading alone feels like more of the same. Trust the process of learning and your ability to see your relationship from a different perspective… that alone may change everything.

Reader's Thoughts

If there was one thing about your own behavior that you'd like to understand, what is it?

How is it affecting your partner?

How is it affecting your life in general?

chapter five

Relationships:
A Reference Framework

Delving into a conversation about how the Hijacked Brain affects relationships is a difficult task. The Hijacked Brain's effect on our emotional experience is one layer; adding to that, how it affects each of the people in a relationship only complicates matters more. To make things just a tad worse, there is the topic of relationships which on its own can be extremely overwhelming—not to use the word *"complicated"* again.

For the purposes of this book, the word "relationships" is defined as a formal construct (marriage, couplehood, committed partnership, etc.) where individuals are working to live and work together toward common goals. Relationships include varying degrees of commitment, emotional investment, and interest in each individual's development and well-being. Our society has given names to our relationships—marriage, partnerships, friendships, etc. While all can be defined as relationships, our observations and work relate to what we call Intimate Relationships. These we further qualify by including exclusivity and sexual interest and interactions.

We propose that intimate relationships are uniquely positioned to either accelerate or hamper our development and well-being in ways and to an intensity level that no other relationship can provide.

We do not present our theories as *THE TRUTH,* but as a lens to be used in order to understand *YOUR TRUTH.*

You may notice that you do not fit one type or another, but rather move from one relationship format to another or from attributes in one format to another. Additionally, the types can be determined developmental in nature, with each being appropriate at different stages of relationship growth. Read through with pause and curiosity.

Our hope is that by the time you've read the separate parts presented throughout the book, their sum, as they apply to your circumstance, will be clear.

Let's start:

Many experts in the field have looked at types of relationships. We have used observations from what has been explained by other experts plus our observations and have come up with three kinds of relationships:

The Glob   The Polar   The Ideal

The Glob

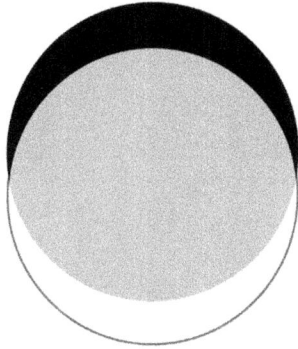

Attributes of *The Glob* include:

- Degrees of obsessive thinking about each other and the relationship
- Inability to experience joy when away from the other
- Unwillingness to develop individual interests
- Belief that the connection is experienced in exactly the same way by both parties
- Inability to argue without taking personal injury
- Magical thinking about what is experienced and what is thought by the other person in the relationship
- Possessive traits

The Glob is characterized by enmeshment. The individuals in this couple seem not to be able to function outside the relationship. Their time is spent with each other, or talking about each other or the relationship. Disagreements are understood as personal injuries and assaults. Expectations of time, interest or relatedness are singular to each other. The individuals in this couple are easy to spot.

**Jane &
Lou**

"Jane, lets go to dinner tomorrow night," says Milly.
"I don't know," says Jane. "I hate to leave Lou by
himself… plus, I just miss him. Maybe another time?"

Developmentally, this is appropriate at the start of a romantic relationship. However as the relationship matures, remaining at this stage can cause:

Loss of identity

Loss of identity is at work when a person is unable to experience their internal world or enjoy the external world without the cooperation or contribution of the other. This is not a state where people linger voluntarily.

**Annie &
Jamie**

Annie brings a piece of fruit home. To her estimation,
this fruit is perfectly ripe and incredibly delicious. She
observes that her pleasure is not complete until she is
able to share the fruit with Jamie. However, Jamie is
not home. Annie feels a knot in her throat and puts the fruit away:
"It's just not enjoyable without him."

Desperate efforts for individualization

If members of a couple insist on staying in the Glob, without a doubt the individuals will experience periods of rebellion, which can take the form of lies, nonsensical disagreements, blown out fights, and even affairs. While many of these affairs can include sex, a great number of them do not include sexual contact. Rather these are emotional connections created with new/other individuals for the sake of finding a space where the member of the couple in question is without their partner. Additionally, the effort to individualize can drive people to substance and pornography use.

A great way to understand this concept is to consider what you would do if someone was holding your head underwater. At some point, you would start splashing and scratching—anything to get a breath. The Glob, if left as such, makes people fight for their lives, consciously if they are aware enough or unconsciously if needed.

Increased frustration towards each other

In a continued effort to individualize, people in this type of relationship begin to nitpick at everything from haircuts to the way a person breathes. The two that could not stand being away from each other are now unable to be in each other's presence. Tenderness moves aside to give way to exasperation and criticism. This makes the couple's ability to move past this stage difficult as the need for understanding and forgiveness becomes a new layer of complication.

Frequent and unexplained deep sense of loss and low self-esteem

At the point of negative culmination to this phase, people report sadness, regret, self-loathing, and, very often, depression. These emotional stages are of no assistance to the struggling couple. Too often by this point people have not only given up on the relationship, but on themselves.

A NOTE: We mentioned above that this is a normal stage in a new couple. So, what makes NORMAL go BAD? We have been able to identify five behaviors, attitudes and ways of being that assist the turning:
- The couple's isolation from other people
- Unwillingness to pursue and/or support each other's pursuit of individual interests
- Rigidity about "things" staying the way they are
- Strict adherence to traditions and beliefs that make it difficult to allow fluidity to the relationship and the people in it
- Reluctance to be fully expressed with the other in the couple

The Polar

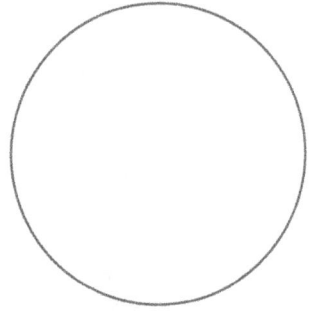

Attributes of *The Polar* include:

- Mutual isolation
- "Busy" is a common excuse for not spending time together
- "Me time" takes priority above "We time"
- Deepest thoughts, ideas and wants are kept hidden
- It is easier to share self with others than with partner
- Respect is lost

While most outsiders may never know, the individuals in this couple value their individuality above their partnership. We have encountered this type in relationships at all stages. It is developmentally appropriate to find this with the advent of children. The couple's schedules are dramatically different, their routines do not include each other, and their interests and responsibilities call them away from each other.

If left unattended, this can become the way things are and the couple enters the therapist's office as children begin school (if they are lucky), but too often they come in as kids go away to college. This, of course, is the worst of all scenarios, but just as common.

These individuals are exposed to:

Feeling isolated

We all talk a big talk about being independent, but the reality is that humans need humans to thrive. Consider this scenario:

You wake up in the morning and look at yourself in the mirror while exclaiming: "Good morning, self! You are awesome and this is going to be an awesome day." You believe the words and head out to complete the tasks for the day...except that throughout the whole day, nobody calls your name, no one looks you in the eye, and nobody acknowledges you or your awesomeness at all.

"Its okay," you say to yourself, and the next day you wake up just as the day before: "Good morning, self! You are awesome and this is going to be an awesome day." A few days go by and you start to notice that you don't believe the words as much and no longer feel the pep they used to give you. Eventually there will be no more "Good morning, self..."

Humans need other humans to witness and share their existence. We need other people to confirm our reality, to mourn our losses, and celebrate our achievements. This we cannot give ourselves, and without it, we wither and die— be that emotionally or physically, we cannot survive alone.

Sometimes, how we look and the effort we put into creating the image we want our partner to see impedes us from stating our desires clearly. This can extend to emotional and sexual needs, which can be difficult to communicate.

Making the decision that our partner cannot handle what we need is a dangerous position to take. The threat is as real to the relationship as a gun to the head would be to an individual. Supposing that we are the only ones morphing in the relationship is neither realistic nor fair. We must remain open and assist each other to do the same. The alternative is unflinchingly committing "relationship suicide."

Avoiding this misstep is simple but difficult, as it requires that we relinquish control and genuinely express ourselves and our desires. We must do so respectfully, void of demands. The receiving partner has the task of remaining open, curious, and supportive while also being genuine.

We have seen this process over and over again. Ricky and Janet's experience illustrate it well:

Janet & Ricky

After 20 years of marriage, Ricky and Janet come for counseling. They are stuck in a rut and seem unable to climb out on their own. Many sessions into the therapeutic engagement, Janet explains, "Sometimes I feel like he is keeping secrets, but when I ask, he says everything is okay." Ricky takes a deep breath and says, "It's not secrets, it's more like fear. I am afraid that if I say what I want or need you will think differently about me, that I will somehow not be good in your eyes. I can't risk that!"

Now, Ricky and Janet were facing a choice: learn each other's truth or retreat into what was known and safe and ignore the statement made by Ricky. We have seen it go both ways: If they choose "not-to-rock-the-boat," neither will be fully satisfied in the relationship and eventually it will not thrive or, worse, it will not survive.

Those who take the risk and expose themselves reap success, and their sacrifice and effort can result in closeness, sexual aliveness, mutual satisfaction, and enhanced life experience.

Depression

If the anecdote above does not serve to explain how a person in this situation can enter a depression, let's add a little more evidence. Nothing affects a person's emotional and psychological well-being more than their intimate relationship. Work can affect us, but if our home life is going well, we will find support and guidance, making the work-related issues bearable. Similarly, if we are dealing with elderly parents or raising children while our intimate relationship is in good shape, the days will be tiring, but there will be a sense of refuge and safety when the night comes and we retreat to spend time with the person who makes it all worthwhile. If our intimate relationship is not providing that kind of support, we are off-kilter and simply unable to manage the difficulties, let alone thrive in them.

Depression is the price we pay for disregarding our emotional and psychological needs as well as the needs of our intimate relationships.

The best way to delve into this situation is to look at Evan and Angela.

After buying a house and having their first child, they lost interest in each other. Angela would have a "girl's night out" and Evan had his art gallery openings to attend. Neither expressed interest in the other's activities nor any other interests, even if they shared those before. They related to each other as "friends with benefits" as opposed to life partners. She stated: "The sex was good, but I started to feel deeply sad after sex. We were so disconnected on things that mattered. He could be anyone now. I could have this kind of sex with anyone and it would not make a difference." Evan agreed, and the work began.

Evan & Angela

Here is what they agreed to do:
- Go on dates regularly. During those dates the conversation was geared towards learning about each other—new books they just read, a new TV show, or a new restaurant was discussed.

- One phone call in the middle of the day just to check in. These were initiated by either of them, and served to show concern—not ask for milk to be bought on the way home.
- Spontaneous love notes, including private messages and innuendo that would make them smile.

Does it sound like too much work? Evan and Angela reported that at the beginning, the efforts felt made-up—forced. But in time, as they gave way to curiosity and interest, love entered the equation and they were both looking forward to the next date, chat, and note.

All too often, work, kids, and other social or community responsibilities become more important than the partner. We hear them say things like: "But this is in the service of the family." Make no mistake and rest assured that no activity, including work, which limits, separates, or alienates a partner serves the relationship or the family.

Take George and Karen.

George & Karen

George was a powerhouse manager already identified and a potential leader at work. His meetings ran late and took him away from home almost every night. Karen, a nurse, worked overnights and insisted that work felt like a vacation, as it kept her from feeling alone at night. Neither was looking to thrive in this relationship. This dynamic is often complicated by a consistent belief that "this is as good as it gets" and that "this good is good enough." However, the individuals report pain, distrust and, more frequently than not, they report no satisfaction or fulfillment is found in the relationship.

The Ideal

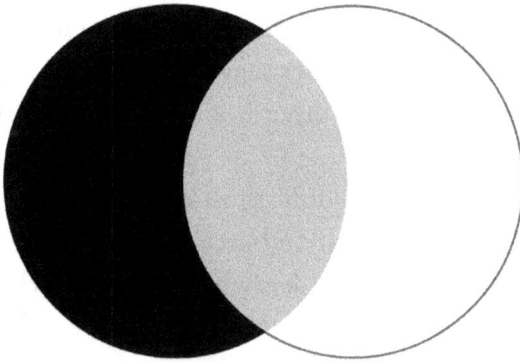

Attributes of *The Ideal* include:

- Supportive & Compassionate
- Open and honest—even when this leads to disagreement
- Allow conversations to disappear and re-start without carry over
- Prioritize time and resources to the benefit of the other and the couple
- Willing to grow and encourage growth
- Confident in their ability to overcome challenges
- See disagreements as opportunities to grow and to learn
- Not a 50/50 but a 100/100 commitment

This is the be-all and end-all of relationships. In this couple, the individuals are fully expressed and fulfilled in their individual lives and with each other. They feel independently whole and thoroughly enjoy sharing their lives with one another. They come together willingly and openly. They refrain from making each other all good or all bad, and understand that they are fluid and capable of all types of behaviors. Behaviors are seen as unique and "of the moment" instead of predictable and directed to the other. They are open to understanding each other's views and opinions, and relish in their collective wisdom. Neither is better than the other and their time apart is fully supported and encouraged.

Integrity rules their individual existence and their mutual commitment colors the choices they make, whether they are together or apart. Trust is eminent, as the well-being of the other is a clear priority. Their communication style includes:

- *Openness*—Even about the difficult issues.
- *Honesty*—Not as an expectation but as a way of being.
- *Genuineness*—They are fully themselves when in each other's presence.
- *Clarity*—Time is taken to say what is meant—hear what is said—and reply in kind.
- *Curiosity*—Nothing is taken for granted and a sense of excitement propels conversations, discussions, and even arguments.

They have found the way to be individuals yet selfless with their partner. They are able to work as a team to balance all aspects of their life together, including children, careers, playtime, friends, etc. The people in this relationship style respect each other and seek to grow individually which, in turn, grows the couple.

Does this seem impossible to achieve? It isn't, but it does require constant willingness to risk our comfort and well-being for the benefit of the relationship.

Being in the ideal relationship is not a matter of arrival, but a process.

Jamie & Annie

When Jamie and Annie first came to therapy, there was no empathy between them. But after about 9 months in therapy, their interactions began to morph in the most unexpected ways. Annie had always begged for closeness and emotional intimacy. Jamie would reply with some version of "What you want would not be natural. I would have to make an effort, and if I have to make an effort it just won't happen..."

During Annie's latest long trip, it occurred to Jamie that he would send flowers to her room so she would find them when she arrived. Annie was both surprised and deeply touched, and communicated to Jamie what this had done for her.

In the past, Annie would have held her appreciation hostage and wondered for as long as she was away what Jamie was trying to cover up or get over on. When we looked at the simple event together, Jamie reported that sending the flowers did take effort, but not of the kind he had feared. Rather, the effort came in responding to an already-present desire to do something nice for Annie.

This was a huge realization for him, as he recognized that he often thought of her and had deep desires to make her smile or make her feel wanted and loved. The trick, he said, was "To act on my thoughts and desires instead of assuming that she already knew what and how I felt."

When Annie examined her own reactions to the flowers, she acknowledged that she accepted the gift on its own as opposed to attached to something else, and was able to express her gratitude in a way that helped them both move closer to each other, even while they were miles apart.

There were ongoing consequences of their realization. Jamie did not feel put upon when he followed up with a feeling or thought about Annie. He found it easy to send texts and make calls, as well as plan in-person and "apart dates" that helped them to nurture each other and help them feel closer. For Annie, there was freedom in openly acknowledging her gratitude, and she felt excited to reciprocate in meaningful and bond-building ways.

Existing in the Ideal is a process. To keep the process going, we must constantly care for ourselves and further our personal growth.

Growth takes:
- Personal awareness
- Taking responsibility for our actions
- Acknowledging our intentions
- Giving up the pursuit to be right
- Valuing the contributions our partner makes in our life
- Nurturing vulnerability
- Asking for and securing help as needed
- Showing gratitude and appreciation
- Admitting when wrong
- Trusting the other

A Point to Ponder:

Even people with excellent mental health cannot assure that they will be able to access, utilize, or be able to behave as required in the list above. It is safe to deduce that individuals struggling with any degree of mental health challenge (even if the challenge is limited to stress) can expect greater difficulty reaching this level of functionality.

Accepting our limitations, recognizing our responsibility, and committing to the process required for growth is imperative in order to bring our behavior and ourselves to a desirable and "connectable" state.

Then, the most logical question at this point is: how is this done? If this is asked in earnest intent, the answer is also logical: we take one thing at a time; we choose that "thing" by looking at areas that are most likely to enhance our relationship and our life in general; and we make a choice and a commitment.

Commitments are dangerous proposals as they not only bring to light that which is important to us, they also bring to light our integrity as it relates to the areas touched by the commitment. Let's dissect that a little further: we tend to only commit to do things we consider important. Too often, the statement of commitment is made without regard to situation, ability, capacity, or the cost of the commitment being made. In romantic relationships, much has to be considered before making and trusting a commitment.

The stage of the relationship:

It is easy to imagine that early on we are all likely to make commitments and work hard to keep them. As time passes and people are less focused on each other but on work, professional growth, children, extended family, etc., the willingness to commit to the relationship decreases. Unless effort is applied, there is no possibility of making or keeping commitments of any kind.

Capacity to live up to commitments:

The wellness and wholeness of each person will affect his/her ability to live up to commitment. The very coping mechanisms that work so well to keep us going will also make it difficult to impossible for us to keep commitments. Humans are complex and layered. The ability to self-observe, name the struggles, and honestly present what we are capable to take on is imperative to making commitments that will be carried through to completion.

The reality of the situation:

Too often, people misrepresent themselves, their wants and needs, as well as their level of commitment to the relationship. Couples would benefit from developing clear definitions to commonly-used words. Particularly important is a joint definition of the word commitment. We cannot assume that the word means the same to everyone. To Kate, commitment may mean "I will do what I said I would, as long as I am not confused—tired—overwhelmed—unhappy." For Tom it may mean "I will keep my commitments as long as I don't have to be vulnerable to do it."

The following definition is offered as a springboard: "We define commitment as a mutual agreement intended to benefit both parties. Commitments are alive and can change."

Take it, internalize it, discuss it with your partner, and make changes until it fits you. The definition can be changed any time; the key here is not to change the rules of the game unilaterally. When the definition to this or any other trigger word does not fit any one person, it is his/her responsibility to come to the table and discuss the new needs.

Carter & Sue

Carter and Sue entered the office with significantly different outlooks. Sue seemed defeated while Carter seemed excited. The story is summarized in the definition of the word commitment. Sue understood it to mean fidelity and monogamy. This definition was not longer suitable for Carter who wanted to be in an open marriage and possibly include other partners to their sexual experiences. After a few months, they both understood that they would not be able to develop a new definition that suited both of them. The therapy was turned to areas that required their conjoint effort (the children) and Carter and Sue were able to dissolve their marriage with no animosity. The children became their focus and each moved on to developing the kind of relationship they found fulfilling.

Yes, the summary of this story seems flat and direct; the process was not. Therapy is rarely a straight line from one place to another. However, the story does highlight the impact of personal awareness, willingness to be vulnerable, clearly understanding when there is no consensus, and the ability to work to honor the other person, even when the marriage is no longer a viable option.

Reader's Thoughts

Where does your relationship fall? The Glob, the Polar, the Ideal?

How do you contribute to the dynamic in your relationship?

How can you start to bring your relationship closer to the Ideal?

chapter six

The Emotional Experience
for Her and Him

"What in the world is happening?"

This is often the question individuals ask when their relationship is impacted by the Hijacked Brain. Sometimes the words people use to describe how they feel are a bit more colorful, but the points they make are one or a combination of the following:

"I thought everything was good and in a moment, it all changed and now I am walking on eggshells."

"Nothing I do is right."

"It feels like a chasm separates us."

"I want to talk about how I feel but I am convinced that no matter what I say, I won't be heard."

"I just get angry…"

"I mean, what's the point of trying to make someone happy when something is obviously wrong, and when I ask what's going on I am made to feel crazy. I either get the look of 'you should know' or the yelling begins with accusations of all the many things I don't do or understand. I am tired."

Each person in a couple is having a unique emotional experience. Each is seeing the world from a specifically-shaped window. This is an important principle, because too often we give in to the belief that others see and feel what we see and feel, which is seldom the case. This is true in good times and in bad times. Intimate relationships are strong catalysts to our worst and best ways of seeing the world; each individual is deeply affected by the other.

Because of the many layers complicating couples' dynamics, we wanted to highlight some commonalities among the individual men and women in couples. Each of their unique experiences gives light to the development of their dynamic.

The Women

These are comments made by women in treatment:

The Blues

"How can I give voice to this experience? Sometimes I wake up and even before my feet touch the floor I feel it. Worse yet, my brain has fully committed to the insistence of negative thoughts. My hair looks awful, nothing fits… but these are relatively easy to manage with a ponytail and a loose dress. But the negativism goes on through the day. It takes

incredible effort just to be pleasant and not just give into the possibility that nothing is going right. Too often, my significant other wants to reason with me. He wants to find a way to FIX IT. But when I am this emotionally spent, I don't need help to make a list of what will make everything better. What I need is a solid ear, an open heart; maybe some reassurance and reminder that I have survived this pit before. The kind of help I am wishing for isn't about what he does, but what he doesn't do. Help, to me, looks like this: he is not in a hurry for me to get over it, he lets me cry without asking me to stop cause 'it isn't that bad'; he is not afraid of my fears... not afraid of me. Sadly, my wish is not likely to come true. I wish it wasn't, but it just has to be difficult to deal with me when I get like that..."

Anger

"Anger is easy to access. When my head is full of negative thoughts and I start thinking people can see it, I get anxious. I wonder what would happen if I could actually tell someone I am afraid they will see how sad I feel... instead, I cover it all up with a sour attitude and choice words. It's the only way I can protect myself. Keep people at bay. Including him... I don't want him to know how I really feel. In all honesty, my anger, at the time, feels real and justified. And having that energy is ne hundred times better than the sadness or the fear.

As you can imagine, the impulsivity to lash out is particularly difficult to overcome. Due to this, unless I am extremely mindful of my emotional state and how I am behaving due to it, this particular symptom can give way to more than a handful of serious fights with my partner. Sometimes, I have enough insight to welcome his "Oh, honey, can we not do this?" and use his comment to redirect behavior or carefully consider my thinking and emotional status. But if it is the end of the day and I have decided that NOTHING is going my way, his comment will for sure be the unneeded spark to a fiery situation.

All I know is that anger feels better than any other emotion."

Fear & Anxiety

These two emotions must be discussed together, because they are so alike and seem to take turns wreaking havoc.

"I can say that when this is my emotional space, I can go from frantic about missing a deadline at work to fearing being fired, even though my work status is secure."

Like "the blues," anxiety has a tendency to populate the content of thoughts while fear feeds the fire. The result is confusion and exhaustion, both discussed below. Additionally, there is the sense of being paralyzed, unable to motivate, move forward or take initiative. Some may think, "What is is the big deal?" but the truth is that a lot can be damaged in a fit of anxiety, and repairing what gets damaged can add to the sense of exhaustion, not to mention the great harm it does to self-esteem.

Confusion

"How can I not be confused? In a matter of hours, I can go from feeling confident and centered to feeling overwhelmed by emotion, annoyed by people, unable to manage behavior to the point of thinking I am ill, and ready to pick a fight with whoever gets in my way. Do I seem crazy to you? The truth is that I am not... I happen to be smart and funny, hardworking and engaging... But when my brain gets hijacked, my internal experience is nothing short of overwhelming. I need respite, and this too is confusing because I can't seem to figure out where to get it. I want closeness but push people away, I feel tired but can't bring myself to rest, and I am overwhelmed but unable to prioritize. Tell me, would you not be confused too?"

Attacked

"In the midst of all this upheaval there is the complication of really believing that people in general, but particularly those closest to me, are out to get me. They push my buttons and they feel like grenades. They deny my claims, and that adds to my anger and confusion. I am unable to trust them or my instincts.

Guilt

"Too often I can tell that my behavior is off... this brings up more of the blues and with them guilt... I should know better, do better. The cycle of emotionality is insidious and all I want is to be out of it!"

Tired

"Exhaustion is a common physical complaint, but I figured out that this is the way I avoid the emotions and the effort it takes to manage behavior. It is the nicest tool during those difficult days to keep people away... and sometimes, it even brings me some compassion... people get it when I say I am tired. They don't get anything else related to my experience."

What's a girl to do?

"With so much going on, it's no wonder that what to do is not obvious. I did not choose to have these emotional experiences, and yet they are mine. I don't want to have my brain hijacked. I don't want to regret things I say or do. Sometimes the best I can do is shrink, but that is only possible when sadness is the only emotion present. If anger is part of the process, shrinking is hard to do."

The Men

Just like women have a way to describe their feelings, so do the men. One of the reasons it is important to address the male's emotional experience is because men traditionally do a good job of keeping their emotions hidden, too often even from themselves. Overtly or covertly, men are taught that showing emotion is a "sign of weakness" and, therefore, the tough guy façade has to be present. There are a few problems with this line of thinking. First, we do not always do a good job of keeping our emotions inside. Often, we may be calculating and measuring what we say and how we act, yet all the while our body language and tone of voice are not able to "hide" what true emotions communicate:

"There is something wrong, but I'm going to pretend otherwise."
"I won't let you see how I feel."
"I don't need you."
"I won't trust you."

...and other sentiments that push women's intuitive buttons.

This leads to the second problem with this thinking: the destructive effect that hiding our emotions has on the relationship. Instead of addressing the emotions head-on and attempting to reverse course, our decision to keep them inside yet display negative body language is known to create conflict. We tend to try and hide, become occupied with something or someone else, and have very minimal contact with our significant other.

Instead of having a discussion about how your own brain was hijacked and bring awareness for her about your needs or thinking patterns, there is now a full-on fight about how you don't share or show emotion, and she always has to be the one to draw information out of you by the teaspoonful. The fight is about something completely different than the real issues, which makes it inefficient, misdirected, and a waste of time and emotion.

Emotional reactions

There are many different emotional reactions experienced by men. The following list is not all-inclusive, yet captures some of the most common experiences reported by our clients. The emotional experiences described are not to be used as excuses for ensuing behavior. Instead, they are a way to recognize and hopefully bring to light the multiple factors that affect the couple's dynamic.

Fix-it:

One of the reactions that men experience strongly is in the way they express understanding and compassion. When men sense that there is a problem, they jump to "solution mode." This is one of the largest communication differences between the sexes. Most women report that they do not want their partner to "find" a solution. In fact, they report that as soon as their significant other goes into "fix-it mode," they are no longer listening or being present with them. Women report that they want their spouse to listen in solidarity and validate the emotions they are experiencing. As one wife stated, "Sometimes I just need you to listen and know that you care."

Anger

This is not always displayed as violent, physical aggression, although there are some instances where that occurs. If that is happening to you, please seek additional assistance immediately as it is never acceptable for physical abuse to occur. The anger referenced here is more in line with the male desire to protect. When men feel their territory or love life is in danger, there is a desire to protect and defend. This is much easier for a male when the "enemy" is seen or physically present, but when there is an emotional attack, men tend to struggle with how to respond. Often the response is to shut down.

Avoidance

One of the most difficult behaviors to identify and overcome is avoidance. Often this is a covert behavior (sometimes even hidden from the person engaged in it). Those who engage in it do so as protection from feeling overwhelmed or are at a loss on how to handle the situation. Some examples include drug and alcohol consumption. When the behavior is questioned we hear reasoning such as "I needed to take the edge off..."

Another avoidance effort we see often is infidelity. The driving force behind this particular behavior is the need of distraction from the turmoil. Affairs as a form of avoidance are directed towards seeking a place of respite; someone to laugh with or have a conversation that is not emotionally charged. Gaming, sports, TV shows, work, and numerous other behaviors are taken on to avoid the difficult reality of not being able to express needs or solve an impasse.

Fear

Truth be told, many men are afraid of their own feelings. Men's emotional experience can be confusing, unclear, and cause a need to figure out what exactly it is they are feeling. Often this is self-preservation to protect oneself from feeling vulnerable—which by all accounts is desirable, but not accessible under these circumstances.

Independence

Men often feel that they must solve problems and issues on their own. They may seek another male friend to bounce ideas off, but still most guys will internalize because they want to be independent thinkers, and ego is increased when problem solving is completed by themselves. The issue is that often humans do best at solving problems—particularly emotion-related problems—with the assistance of others. Because men tend to bottle up and try to solve issues internally, the common consequence is frustration from all sides.

Janet and Ricky illustrate the cycle well:

Janet & Ricky

Ricky was overwhelmed at work. The pressure to meet a deadline was mounting and he had lost a few workers. The issues were going on for some time, but he had not mentioned any concerns to Janet. So, he was carrying on with routines as usual; picking up and dropping off the kids, attending games, and assisting with needed tasks and chores. Janet had picked up on his tension and asked what was going on and if there was anything she could do. Ricky would deny her intuitive question and even diminish her concerns: "What are you talking about? I am fine—What am I doing that makes you ask that?" One afternoon he comes in the house actively angry. He pushes things with his feet; his mood is undeniable. "Ok, really? What is going on?" asks Janet. "Nothing! Nothing is going on," he yells. "Just life going along as if I can do it all. My customers want things done on time, the kids have to be picked up and dropped off on time, and so they are..." He bangs the door and leaves the house. Janet is angry—"How many times can ask what is going on? I am not a mind reader and I too have to meet other people's expectations... What, he thinks he is the only one?"

Attacked

Often, characteristics of communication in the Hijacked Brain consist of quick temper, belittling, inconsistencies, mocking and anger. When these are experienced, there can be a tendency to feel attacked. Due to many factors, including heredity, culture, upbringing, and more, men may respond with anger. This anger will come naturally for men as a defense mechanism. We're not saying it is right, but when attacked, the male response is to respond in one of the few ways they know.

Failure

As the woman, you will probably not see this reaction, but the men will understand. When communication is not going well, and the woman we love is not happy (particularly with us); when we cannot make everything right and aren't able to solve the "problem," then we have a tendency to feel as though we have failed. These feelings of failure can lead to withdrawal from the situation so that we do not make it worse or keep talking in the hopes that we will make it right. Usually neither of these responses works well.

Guilt

Guilt is closely related to failure. There is guilt that men can experience because they did not do enough or well enough in order to maintain a happy, satisfied, content emotional baseline for the woman they love. At this point the desire is to share with the woman how he feels but often this discussion is withheld out of fear that it will do further damage and may cause an increase in the already discord relationship.

Tired

We have all experienced the emotional and physical drain that occurs when interacting with someone whose mood, thoughts, and emotions are inconsistent. This can be in the form of emotional tiredness, when you just feel like you have nothing left to give because it will not be right or interpreted wrongly. Physically your body becomes worn down because so much energy has been spent trying to do the right thing or not do the wrong thing that there is not energy left for other—perhaps stress-reducing—activities. Mentally you become tired to the point where you are preoccupied with trying to "fix" the problem in this relationship that work and other relationships suffer.

Frustration

We all want to be happy. There are very few people who truly want to feel confused, insecure, and shocked in their relationships. Those that do typically do not stay in relationships long. Frustration can set in when men just do not know what to do anymore. When we've tried everything that we know, we have sought guidance and advice, tried doing what we've been told by our significant other and it's still not working, frustration occurs. Unfortunately, the outcomes of frustration do not always look pretty. These reactions can lead to further divide and separation in the moment that does not need any more help.

Guarded and protective

Most people do not want to experience emotional pain, especially from someone they love. When the Hijacked Brain is unleashing its full fury, you may see many men retreat emotionally and physically. This is often a subconscious defense mechanism in order to protect the guy; an opportunity to retreat, gather his thoughts and decide what is the best way to respond. Do not misunderstand: this is not always a guy's first response, but often if you feel like he has become distant it is because of this need to find protection and remove himself from a situation in which he does not feel comfortable, and does not know how to respond quite yet.

What's a guy to do?

Now that we have addressed many of the reactions and responses that a man experiences related to the Hijacked Brain, what can he do? First, there are many tools and resources listed throughout the book and gathered in Chapter Ten: *Resources and Tools*. Review those to see what will work for you. Remember, there is not a "magic pill" or one quick fix that you can use all the time. Instead, the resources are designed to increase the skills in your tool box so that when you experience the Hijacked Brain at other times, in other situations, you have skills with which to respond in a positive, safe way.

Second, we want to spend time here talking specifically about how men and women communicate, which might shed light on how to respond in all situations better. We'll go deeper into communication in another chapter and include specific resources, but this will give you a brief overview of the communication style of you and your significant other. If you can identify your own communication style and that of your significant other, then that awareness will help your future interactions.

Communication styles

Did you know that you are constantly communicating? Some think that only when you speak is communication happening but actually the majority of communication occurs with your body—your non-verbal language. As you read through these styles, think of what communication style you are and the style of your significant other.

Aggressive:

This is a very selfish style of communicating. Essentially it says that it's "all about me!" The person who utilizes this style is all about winning every argument and demonstrating how superior they are to others. Often whatever message they are trying to convey is lost because of their delivery style. This style is characterized by being loud and threatening. They come across as demanding and abrasive. Others often see them as intimidating and bullying. They will use sarcasm, name-calling and insulting language to make their point. Their non-verbal language will include an intimidating posture, large gestures, facial expressions of glaring or scowling, and often they will try to invade others' personal space to intimidate. Those on the receiving end of an aggressive communicator will often feel defensive, resentful, humiliated, degraded, and afraid. There is often a loss of respect for the aggressive person.

Passive:

This style is characterized by a sole desire to please others. Essentially this style of communication believes that others are more important and have more value than themself. They will do anything they can to avoid conflict often by apologizing for everything, yielding to others' preferences and desires, refusing to accept a compliment because they feel they do not deserve and playing the role of the victim. Individuals who communicate this way have a difficult time making or sharing their desires and speaking up for themselves. Their non-verbal communication is often characterized by a low, soft voice, an attempt to make themselves physically as small as possible, no eye contact and being submissive in their actions (doing what they are told without question). Others communicating with a passive style will often feel frustrated, like they can control you, resent the passivity, be annoyed with the lack of confidence, and exasperated.

Passive-aggressive:

You may not know it from the look on the outside but this style of communication is very angry. Individuals who communicate in a passive-aggressive manner will often be acting out their anger behind the scenes in order to harm or sabotage the other person. They often feel resentful or powerless and therefore they may act with sarcasm, complain, sulk, gossip and be devious. The passive-aggressive non-verbal language will often include a soft, sweet voice and facial expressions and often try to appear as being warm and friendly. However, others will often see them as "two-faced" and be confused, angry, and hurt by their inconsistent actions.

Assertive:

The healthiest, most successful communication style is assertive. This is the perfect balance between aggressive and passive. When we are assertive we have the confidence to communicate without feeling like we need to control or manipulate someone. We are able to effectively communicate what we are thinking and feeling while taking into account others' needs. When we communicate assertively, we are protective and respectful, take responsibility for our actions, and are able to ask clearly and directly regarding our needs... fully accepting the possibility that the answer may be no. Non-verbal language includes a controlled volume of speech, relaxing posture that is inviting and non-threatening, good eye contact, and respectful boundaries. Others will experience a sense of trust, respect, and confidence that the information being shared is to benefit them, especially if a critique.

Please note that being assertive does not mean that you will always get what you want. It means that you can accurately and with respect communicate how you feel and what your needs are to another person. Sometimes you will get what you want, sometimes there will be a compromise, and sometimes the answer will be no; regardless, your motives and intentions have been pure and you will have taken responsibility for the way you communicate.

Responding to his experience

Men, hopefully in this chapter you have been able to identify some of the reactions you experience. Truth is, we all experience many of the emotional reactions, often at the same time. While experiencing these temporarily is not a bad thing, they cannot and should not be the norm for how you always respond. If one of these emotional reactions has become your baseline or how you feel most of the time, then it's time to seek professional assistance.

Learning your communication style will help you identify the role that you play in all your relationships. After self-reflection you might find that you communicate a different style with different people or situations. Your goal should be assertive communication in all situations, as this will be the most effective and successful approach to share your wants and needs. Communication that displays support, honor, humility, and respect will allow the conversation to stay on topic and both individuals to feel valued and important. By recognizing the style of others, you can help them become more assertive if needed and be aware of how their style of communicating impacts you.

Ladies, this chapter was designed to have value for you as well, maybe more so than the men. To provide a glimpse into the world of the man's mind and emotional reactions is important knowledge to have. You may have witnessed or been on the receiving end of many of the emotional reactions mentioned. Note they are not to be used as an excuse for abusive behavior and never should be accepted as "that's just the way I am." Everyone is capable of changing their behaviors so that communication is not disrespectful, threatening, or intimidating.

You can play a large role in helping men become more assertive in their communication which will alleviate much of the guessing you do when it comes to what a man is thinking and experiencing. Be aware of the characteristics of each emotional reaction and how it makes him feel. Study your communication style and address areas where you need to work to become more assertive. Imagine a relationship that focuses on open, honest, assertive communication that allows both of you to share what you are thinking, need and want without the fear of guilt, and repercussions associated with your previous interactions. It may open new doors of intimacy you have never imagined.

Reader's Thoughts

Did you find yourself in any of the experiences?

What is different for you?

chapter seven

Intimate Compassion Fatigue

As we've seen with our couples throughout the book and the hundreds of couples and individuals with whom we have worked, relationships are hard. Anytime you are interacting with another person, you have the opportunity to experience many wonderful things such as love, sharing, intimacy, growth, and pain that brings you closer. However, intimate relationships go through cycles, like all relationships that include the bad or tough times with the good times. If more difficult times continue or perhaps are few but very intense when they do occur, we suggest that you can experience intimate compassion fatigue in your relationship.

What is intimate compassion fatigue?

Compassion fatigue has been around for many decades, first being identified in health care professionals and first responders or where there is a great need of having to care for other people. The easiest way to think of compassion fatigue is when someone starts to lose the ability to show compassion. This does not happen quickly but over long periods of time as these helpers continue to be exposed to trauma and stress. We start to see symptoms like stress, anxiety, hopelessness and a decrease in pleasurable activities.

Essentially, you become emotionally tired when you are supporting someone who has been through a tough time. Often we take on their feelings and reactions as our own and, thus, we become fatigued from trying to help.

Intimate compassion fatigue is a new concept that we are introducing. Let's define it like this and then look at an example:

Intimate compassion fatigue
The emotional strain within a relationship when behaviors, emotions and communication are inconsistent with each other. Intimate compassion fatigue occurs over the course of time with continued exposure to the inconsistencies without the experience of alignment between behavior and emotional stance.

Alyssa & Trevor

Trevor and Alyssa have been married for seven years. Alyssa had been on a birth control pill during the early years of their relationship and Trevor rarely knew when her menstrual cycle was occurring. However, Alyssa has been off the pill for four years as they began to plan their family. Trevor started to notice that Alyssa's behavior towards him took a drastic change in the days prior to the start of her cycle. Trevor tried to address it a few times, but Alyssa would become very defensive and blame Trevor for his insensitivity and lack of communication. Trevor, wanting to avoid those conversations, decided not to address it any further, but over the course of time has come to dread that time of the month and actively tries to avoid Alyssa in attempts to "not fight." Trevor tends to work later during this week, has become resentful because he feels he has done "nothing wrong" and is seeing where his feelings for Alyssa during these few days have started to carry over to the rest of their relationship. He started out trying to be compassionate and understanding, but is now tired and avoidant of the situation, not seeing where it will change since Alyssa does not want to address the issues.

What does intimate compassion fatigue look like?

There are many signs and symptoms that you might experience when dealing with intimate compassion fatigue. See if you have experienced any of the following:

- Tired emotionally, physically, and spiritually
- Confused about what happened and where to go next
- Withdrawn; just want to get away
- Inability to focus or concentrate
- Exhausted but cannot sleep
- Insecure about the next encounter
- Feeling hopeless that the situation is going to change
- Feeling helpless; that you are in this by yourself
- Hungry but nothing sounds good; don't want to eat
- Everything annoys you
- Frustrated with inconsistencies
- Disappointed in yourself and your partner
- Short-tempered, always feeling like you are on edge
- Animosity

This is not an all-inclusive list, because we all experience intimate compassion fatigue a little differently. However, it is very important that you do not brush it off or pretend like it does not bother you. Look at that list again and add your own personal reactions. None of what we experience when this happens is positive. As mentioned above, it takes a physical, emotional, and spiritual toll. You may think you are a master when it comes to hiding your reactions but—and here comes the shock—you are not that skilled. Even those of us trained to understand emotional reactions are not able to hide our own. Your intimate partner, kids, friends, family, co-workers—they all will see that something is wrong; you will be the first to know but the last to admit.

Let's pull out a few of the reactions on the list above and go deeper into how intimate compassion fatigue makes you feel and what it does to you over the long haul.

Confused

Remember, the fatigue occurs because there are times in the relationship when all is going well followed by intense periods when "all hell has broken loose." Things you say and do during good times are met with intense negativity during the bad times. Everything you try to do and say does not work and you are left throwing your hands up in confusion.

Withdrawn

Some will want to fight and try to make your intimate partner see that you are right and that their behavior is wrong. However, for the rest of us (and when the fighting does not work) the time comes when you feel so beaten down that you just want to escape. You want a break, something different, a chance to re-energize. We try to find that through staying at work longer or diving into another form of escape, but it's only temporary and will not fulfill the need you have to actually get away. Plus, your intimate partner will know what you are trying to do and most likely it will become an issue.

Exhausted but no sleep

You are tired, so very tired. There is no energy to do anything and you feel like you could sleep for days, yet you lay down your head and your mind is consumed with the issues in the intimate relationship and how everything else is being impacted. If you do sleep for a few hours, it is not restful and you wake up still longing for rest. Day after day of this takes its toll to where your work, taking care of the kids, and all other responsibilities become impacted because you barely have the energy to do the minimum.

Insecure about what happens next

We've all been there: it's been a difficult interaction, with words being said that were hurtful, or body language that just said, "I don't like you." Instead of it being worked out right then and there, the conversation just ended but you know the next interaction is not going to be pleasant. You are unsure what to do, how to act, or what to say because you know it will be wrong. So, we walk on eggshells, waiting for the next blowup. Either way, we expect that there will be a bad outcome or we are not confident in our ability to change the result.

Feeling helpless

When you are in the pits of intimate compassion fatigue, it feels like you are there by yourself. You know that friends or others have probably experienced something similar, but two things happen: (1) you do not want to admit that you feel this way to anyone; (2) you are not even sure of the words to say that would accurately explain what you feel.

You are not on an island. Everyone, including your intimate partner, has experienced this form of compassion fatigue at one time or another. Sharing with someone close can be very helpful, even therapeutic, so that you have a sounding board and others can help. You might just find that their similar experiences can shed new light in a way you never thought.

Annoyed at everything

You know when this happens... everything annoys you: people at the grocery store, co-workers, sports teams, the weather, and definitely other drivers. Most days, what other people do you can brush aside, but when you are in the midst of intimate compassion fatigue, every relationship irritates you to the point where it feels like it just won't stop! You become short-tempered with everyone and expect that there will be no good interactions. You go into a mode of just getting what you need from that person and then move on before they ask you any stupid questions that will annoy you more. Being fatigued with your intimate partner can have this kind of impact on all your other relationships. Be aware of what you are feeling and with whom you are having the real issue before it impacts all of the other relationships in your life.

Frustrated at inconsistencies

This spills over into several of the other reactions, but is worth additional mention. The frustration comes from what we see as the "roller coaster." For the most part, roller coasters are fun, exciting, and thrilling as you anticipate the next drop or turn. In an intimate relationship, the roller coaster ride is not so much fun. We don't always know when the next turn or drop is coming and, therefore, it is hard to prepare. You may think an upswing in the relationship has occurred only to see the bottom drop out over something that seems insignificant. These inconsistencies in the stability of the relationship can cause a great deal of frustration. Prolonged exposure to inconsistencies is not healthy for any relationship and can cause issues of trust.

Disappointment

At this point, you know what's coming, how your partner is going to act, or what will be said, and you know how you should respond but then...you do the opposite. Whether it be pride, control, selfishness or something else, we tend to exaggerate the situation, which just makes it worse. Afterward, you know that your words and actions should have been different. You question how you responded and realize, "I should have done better." You become disappointed in yourself, but there is also disappointment with your intimate partner because you believe they should know better, they should know what to say and how to act. Be careful. Disappointment leads to resentment, and that is definitely not a place for any relationship to stay.

Short-tempered

We have a colleague who will quite often point out when someone is being snarky. Being snarky, or sarcastic, is one of the best forms of being short-tempered that we possess in our communication tool bag. How often do we get little digs in based on what someone has said or done? Some of us are the master of one-liners which do nothing more than add fuel to a simmering fire that can lead to a roaring blaze. But being short-tempered is more than just being snarky. When we are experiencing intimate compassion fatigue, we are often short-tempered in all our relationships. We are not as patient as usual with others and may be quick to criticize with harsh language when softer, encouraging words are available. Being short-tempered shows that you are struggling with self-control, and in an intimate relationship it is important to be mindful of your partner. Your partner's needs are just as important as yours, and finding an appropriate way to communicate those needs are the key to success.

Animosity

Hopefully, we never get to the point where we wish ill or have come to loathe our intimate partner, and yet in reality there are times when it does happen. These are extreme reactions, but when you have experienced the prolonged exposure to all the other responses, one is definitely walking down the path of animosity. This is the worst place you can be as a couple, because at this point you most likely have given up hope and feel like there is no other option but to split as so many other couples have.

But there is hope!

I have intimate compassion fatigue, now what?

If you have read the above and come to the conclusion that you experience intimate compassion fatigue, please do not feel like all is lost even if you have been walking down this path for a very long time. Remember, the goal of this book is to encourage you and your intimate partner and provide tools (see below) that you can use to lead you to the fulfilling relationship you both desire.

Here are some thoughts regarding what you can do to address intimate compassion fatigue:

Exercise

You probably hear that exercise is the key to everything; however, it is very important. With proper and regular exercise you will have a tendency to feel better physically and emotionally. The chemicals released during exercise help you to relax and sleep better.

Hobbies

You have to make time for something that you enjoy. If you find that your intimate relationship is struggling right now (and impacting many other areas of your life), you need something that you can call your own and that brings you enjoyment. Find anything: games, knitting, reading, Netflix, stamp collecting. Anything that brings you joy and satisfaction will be important to maintain.

Humor

Remember all the joy killers listed above? Humor is a great trait that will help you see the world in a different way. If you are struggling in your intimate relationship, do not go see a movie about a couple that has problems; instead, watch your favorite comedy and laugh again.

Self-awareness

Know what pushes your buttons and learn how to change your reactions. Be aware of what your needs are and the realistic ways of getting those needs met. Realize that your body, mind, and emotions are speaking to you and letting you know that special attention is needed at times. You do not need to isolate and always maintain an "I'm fine" posture. That will surely cause you issues when change happens.

Live in reality

This means do not pretend things are good if they are not. Acceptance of real-life circumstances is vital so that you do not try to convince others and—more importantly—yourself of a false reality. Instead of denying where you are, engage your circumstances and look for solutions to the problems before you. One way to do this is by being mindful of where you are, how you are feeling, and the context of the present reality. Also, try being mindful of what experiences your intimate partner is having. This degree of mindfulness will help you see the world through their eyes.

Be flexible

Be flexible in realizing that you will not have all the answers. Men and women think differently, but most of us want to solve problems and enjoy the excitement of finding the answer to a perplexing issue. However, there is nothing more humbling and freeing than being able to say, "I don't know the answer," followed by, "...but I want us to work together to find one."

Learn that there is "no box"

We've all heard the phrase to "think outside the box." Well, when it comes to solving a problem with your intimate partner, you will need to have an unlimited supply of solutions. You will need to consider all possibilities; even ones that may not have worked in the past might work now. Problem solving together includes beginning at "Let's throw all options on the table," regardless of past history or how unorthodox they might seem. Sometimes those are the best solutions.

Write

You may have heard this called journaling; it's the same concept. When you are able to write down what you are thinking and feeling, it acts as a release and frees your mind. When this happens, you are able to get the thoughts that continue to control your every moment on paper (or computer) and, thus, you give yourself a reprieve. By getting out the negative thoughts, you open the door for positive thoughts to enter and gain a new perspective on your current situation.

Learn how to communicate

This may be the most important action you can take; in fact, we think it to be such a huge issue that we have devoted a whole section on communication. We all communicate, but that does not mean that we are all effective at it. We need to have the confidence in our choice of words, timing, and place that we will communicate. Learning how to read body language and respond without being defensive is a skill that everyone needs to have. If you learn how to effectively share your thoughts, feelings, needs, and wants with your intimate partner and, in turn, be able to hear their sharing, you will automatically experience positive steps in healing your relationship and overcome intimate compassion fatigue.

A word about codependency

At this point, it is important that we talk about codependent relationships, as the topic fits well in this discussion of intimate compassion fatigue and the two require distinguishing. Many of you have heard the term codependent. Let's make sure you understand what a codependent relationship is before deciding if you are currently in a codependent relationship:

A one-sided relationship that is emotionally destructive and sometimes abusive. It impacts both partners' ability to have a healthy, satisfying relationship due to the unequal distribution of emotions.

One partner typically gives and sacrifices in order to emotionally maintain the other partner who rarely, if ever, returns the same level of intimacy.

Shawn Burn, Ph.D, states that in a codependent relationship "much of the love and intimacy in the relationship is experienced in the context of one person's distress and the other's rescuing or enabling." There is much to this statement: you know if the role played in your intimate relationship is one that is always rescuing your mate, then you either resent your partner for being in that position or you have found some value and worth in being the only one who can rescue them.

The role of dysfunction

Historically, we think of codependency as the wife enabling her alcoholic husband. While this is where the term originated, the concept can be seen in several types of relationships, including where addiction, mental illness, and any form of dysfunction is present. Now, you might be saying to yourself that every relationship has some form of dysfunction. While that is most likely true, it's the impact of the dysfunction that defines the relationship. Examples of these dysfunctions are:

- Addictions: drugs/alcohol/opioids; sex; shopping; gaming and gambling
- Physical and emotional illness that has significant impact on the relationship
- Abuse that can be in the form of emotional, sexual, physical, or financial

A dysfunctional family or relationship can usually be identified easily by outsiders; however, members will often not acknowledge there is a problem. This is the family that does not trust other family members and certainly does not acknowledge that a problem exists. Instead of the positive acts of love, kindness, patience, gentleness, and understanding, there is often a repression of feelings, thus causing resentment, detachment, hurt, denial, and avoidance. In a sense, they have just learned how to survive the day.

We have been asked many times how a dysfunctional family or co-dependent relationship begins. There are many ways, but often the roots start early on in childhood. Instead of you as the child receiving nurturing, attention, and loving guidance from your parents, you are often having to provide for your parents. This is not financial support (although that can come later when you are an adult), but instead you provide the emotional needs for your parent. This can happen for many reasons such as in single-parent homes, having an absent parent, divorce, death of a parent, alcoholic/substance use in parents, and other situations. Regardless of the reason, the parent has become unreliable or unavailable to provide for the emotions you need as a child.

When this occurs, the child is now put in a position where they are providing for the parent's needs. They learn to make excuses for their parent, take a larger role in offering forgiveness, demonstrate a level of patience they may not understand and, unfortunately, grow up faster than they should. Because they have not had the chance to develop maturity at a normal pace, it is very common for resentment and disappointment to occur. The child can get lost in what they need or want because they have to focus on their parent and they lose a bit of their own identity.

Because they have absorbed that this is what "normal" relationships look like, when the child becomes an adult and seeks an intimate relationship, they look for a similar pattern: someone they can control, rescue, or provide for because this is how they have learned to love and be loved.

Karen &
George

Karen was the oldest in her family of origin. After her father left, her mother became uninterested in the children. The mother's disinterest showed up in many forms, including forgetting to pick the kids up from school or not having groceries in the house. Karen (then 14) took on caring for her siblings and, in many ways, her mom. During treatment, Karen realized she had unwittingly transferred that way of relating to her life with George who, while not neglectful, was definitely distracted. Karen wanted to find a different way to feel and express love and committed to learning to take care of herself—getting clear on her needs and learning to ask what she needed from George.

Survival

In codependent relationships the ability to survive becomes the primary goal. You are certainly not thriving in this kind of relationship! So what does survival look like? Perhaps you relate to one or more of the following:

- You feel trapped in the relationship
- You have a very hard time saying no to the demands of your partner
- The relationship seems based on conditional love or controlling behaviors
- You constantly feel like you are being taken advantage of
- You make extreme sacrifices to meet the partner's needs
- You try to take on your partner's pain in order to relieve them of consequences they have earned
- The way you communicate is unfair, with inappropriate boundaries
- You give more than you get in return
- How others see you is your main worry
- You have a lost sense of who you really are: lost interest, desires, and dreams
- The partner's happiness has become your priority
- You have become a master at making excuses for your partner's behavior
- You will do anything to avoid an argument, including staying quiet

There may be many more examples that you could add, but the point is made: this type of relationship is not healthy and could continue to become worse, especially as the resentment begins to grow because your needs and wants are not being met.

What a healthy relationship looks like for a codependent

When you decide that you are ready to try a different path in your relationship, there are a few things that will start to occur.

First, you will stop allowing yourself to be abused. This includes all forms of abuse that you might be receiving but that you are also doing.

Second, there will be a change in the way you see situations. This is where a focus on your needs and wants starts to occur, and realizing that you are a person who has desires and dreams and—to borrow a Harry Potter term—the dementors cannot take those away from you anymore.

Next, the way you love is defined differently. When you care for someone or do something for them, it is not because you want to control them but because you genuinely love them and are not trying to gain power, control, or so they "owe" you. Relationships become defined by demonstrating love, peace, joy, patience, goodness, kindness, faithfulness, gentleness, and self-control.

Another change will be that you respond instead of react to what others do. Up until this point, your life has been defined by how you react to people…in essence, feeling like you have to do something in response to their actions. As you change, there is a sense of responding that occurs. Responding includes boundaries. Instead of a quick action on your part to everything someone else says or does, you now choose when or if you are going to respond and what that action might be. One of the biggest pieces to success of this step is your ability to accept "no" and say "no". Once you are able to establish the word "no" in your vocabulary, it will be life-altering.

These changes do not happen overnight. Remember that getting to this point or being in this situation is a culmination of many factors, but that does not mean you have to keep the status quo. You are taking a great first step by reading this book, which is education and learning about where you have been. Many of the other resources that we have mentioned will help you as well, including trainings, therapy, group support, and other opportunities that will help you see yourself, others and the world differently.

Reader's Thoughts

What did you discover in this chapter?

What can you put into practice right away?

Take the Intimate Compassion Fatigue Assessment on Pages 125-126

chapter eight

Communication

Communication is possibly the single most telling evidence of a successful relationship. Communication is also the fastest route to improve, heal, restore, maintain, and nurture relationships. Without communication, individuals wither away and, with them, their relationships.

We define effective communication as the open and honest interchange springing from curiosity, and supported by respect, which expands and nurtures mutual interest.

For the purpose of this book, we define communication within a couple as an ongoing interchange of ideas, thoughts, and opinions. Communication takes place through words, tone, body language, and presence. These elements are then combined with our conscious and even unconscious *intention* producing a message that is then *interpreted* by the other person(s).

Intention and interpretation are important parts of communication that are too often dismissed and not even acknowledged. But these powerful parts determine much of what is said and understood.

Successful Relationships

A couple is not deemed successful because it stays together. It is successful because the individuals in it grow and live lives of integrity with a concern for self that does not harm the other.

Intention—Our "Come From"

Intention is often unconscious but fuels much of what we feel, how we express ourselves, what we defend and fight for; in essence, intention is the birthplace of how and what we choose to communicate. On the other side of communication, intention colors what we hear and how we perceive what is being said; it colors interpretation. Communication is never one-faceted. To insist that it is denies and obscures powerful forces at play in all interactions.

Because of its powerful influence, acknowledging and understanding our "come from" will allow us to be clearer in our messaging.

In intimate relationships, we are exerting efforts to resolve multiple layers of issues—some current, such as the issue the couple may be discussing; some related to emotional expenditure such as yesterday's disagreement while driving home; worries about today's challenges at work; concerns over ailing loved ones; the list goes on and on. Some are long-term psychological issues—am I good enough, I have or need to win, am I lovable. We are not constantly aware of all that is affecting the accordion of intentions igniting a comment. However, it is possible for us to become aware of the themes that matter to us and are likely to color our words, behavior and understanding.

Reaching a high level of honesty about our own intention (see the section on self-awareness) can be difficult, and many say it is scary... difficult because our intention morphs over time, and changes with topic, the people involved, stage of life we are in and other factors; it is scary because too often the truth about our intention does not match our self-identification or description.

Identifying our intention or "come from" requires that we:

- Be in touch with our emotional reactions and give them fitting names
- Question what is causing the emotional reaction (clue: it is never what the other person said)
- Investigate how deeply rooted is the cause of the reaction

While working with a therapist to reach this level of self-understanding is highly recommended, other activities such as meditation, free flow writing, and mindfulness practices can be effective in giving access to intentions.

NOTE: while reaching and working through unconscious intentions is desirable, much progress can be made by naming and addressing conscious ones. Knowing that we want the next words we say to be as hurtful as possible can give access to a higher level of self-control or a new way to express the importance of the issue at hand.

What makes the uncovering of hidden intentions scary is that they are obscured to us by a psychological effort to protect ourselves. Finding out that we take pleasure in hurting a loved one is not likely to be a welcome realization. The more deep-rooted a hidden intention is, the more having a trained therapist guiding the process matters.

Interpretation, or "Understanding the Other"

Intimate relationships are working fields for our most intimate personal struggles and those struggles affect our interpretations.

Communication is never more important or relevant than in an intimate relationship. Intimate relationships provide a space where so much depth can be shared, but also where the impact of emotions and past experiences greatly influence the deciphering of messages or the meaning we give to what the other person says.

Interpretation is greatly affected by unresolved history. A disagreement can ensue over ice cream and have NOTHING to do with ice cream and everything to do with a situation long ago that involved getting or not getting something we wanted. Our defense mechanisms are so strong that we buy into the idea that the issue is the ice cream.

We fall into this kind of personal delusion as an avoidance strategy—this is true—but the delusion will not move us closer to resolving the past or current issue; it will not nurture the relationship and will not promote personal growth. In order to be sure that what we understand is in fact what is being said, all involved must *practice curiosity*, the willingness to *take risks*—meaning be vulnerable, and must let go of *the need to be right*.

Effective communication is not limited by anyone's current abilities; if we allow ourselves the opportunity to be introspective, and then given our observations make adjustments to our style and approach, the transformation of our selves and our relationship(s)—of any kind—is within reach.

Barriers to Communication and Ways to Address Them

There are many barriers that impact our ability to communicate effectively. Intention and interpretation can be some of them (see above). Some others are:

- Personal Stances
- Interpersonal Opinions
- Language
- Cultural Differences
- Family of Origin Impact

Personal Stances

Personal stances are fueled by our individual beliefs and our values. Beliefs are thoughts that we hold as true; for example, "Blue is the best color." Values are thoughts that we hold as important—even non-negotiable; for example, "Self-respect is a must for all humans."

When beliefs and values converge a personal stance is born; for example, a personal stance born from the belief and value shown above may be: "All self-respecting persons wear blue." A personal stance gives way to how we perceive, speak, and interpret. There is nothing inherently wrong with having personal stances; it is our reliance on them and fierce belief in their absolute correctness that causes conflict.

Some of the most common personal stances brought in by couples are:

- I am right
- I know better
- My way or the highway
- Keeping score

While it is impossible to outline the possible beliefs corroborating each of these stances, identifying the values that fuel them is an easier task. Here are possible values fueling the most common stances:

I am right
- Assertiveness
- Decisiveness
- Fortitude
- Mastery
- Order
- Purpose
- Recognition
- Results Oriented
- Self-Reliance
- Vision

I know better
- Accountability
- Boldness
- Certainty
- Competition
- Control
- Effectiveness
- Efficiency
- Responsibility
- Stability

My way or the highway
- Accuracy
- Capable
- Certainty
- Determination
- Excellence
- Ferocious
- Intensity
- Leadership
- Success
- Thorough

Keeping score
- Ambition
- Balance
- Consistency
- Equality
- Fairness
- Integrity
- Justice
- Logic
- Order
- Power
- Victory

Notice that the values are not negative in nature. Believing that what motivates OUR behavior is THE best or RIGHT or ONLY motivator is the cause of the problem.

Being Right

One of the most commonly found opinions and a great human mis-conception is "I am Right." The permutations of this stance are infinite, but can be boiled down to these untruths:

1. *My reality is REALITY*—A global delusion and yet not centered on anything "REAL". To assume that others see and experience the world or a situation the way we do omits that they have a different perspective and a right to that perspective. Reality is uniquely individual. We gain more through curiosity about an-other's view than by imposing our view.

2. *The way I think and what I believe is THE TRUTH*—If the truth is limited to what I know or believe, then there is no need for research of any kind, learning is irrelevant, and growth is neither possible nor desirable. People have access to truth—their truth. To hold on to ours as the ONE and ONLY refuses and even rebukes theirs.

3. *My common sense IS "Common Sense"*—As Voltaire put it, "The thing about common sense is that it is not so common." Under-standing and expressing our perspective and position as A posi-tion instead of THE position allows for freedom of expression from all parties.

4. *Others should think the way I think and if they don't they are wrong*—Humans are comfortable in familiar places, situations and relation-ships. Facing someone with a different frame of mind or thinking pattern can feel foreign, even threatening. We tend to avoid foreign things, missing the fact that in the foreign lies The New, The Oppor-tunity, The Possibility, The Lesson, The Learning, The Difference that can cause us to see and behave differently. The great challenge here is to learn to hold the ambiguity that right and wrong do not have exclusive existence. We can both all be right and wrong at the same time, at the same measure, or about the same thing.

5. *Explaining myself is a senseless practice*—Avoiding the effort to explain ourselves is unfortunate for all involved. In processing an explanation, we often get clear about our own position and with a little effort the beliefs and values that support our thinking. The process of explaining oneself requires vulnerability—possibly the most important ingredient to intimacy and closeness.

Giving up our need to be right is a requirement to understanding messages others are sending our way. It is also necessary in order to create bonds, grow, and properly communicate our thoughts and needs to others.

I Know Better

"I know better" could be positioned as a function of "I am right." However, there is a distinction that separates this category—the persistent notion that our contribution is of higher value than anyone else's. Some of the most common telltales of this opinion is the report of feeling controlled. Whether the concerns are financial, children, cultural, spiritual, or even entertainment-related, if we insist that we know better the result is a disappearing partner and ultimately a disintegrating couple.

Recognizing that we hold the opinion that "we know better" begins the process of dislodging the stance. However, we are resistant to the shift and will often deny the need to let go. "I know better" has its foundation in the need for control and anxiety about the unknown, hence the resistance. As long as the individuals in a relationship see each other as a responsibility-liability-or-reflection of self, elevating them to partner-contributor-or-collaborator is unlikely.

When we allow ourselves to see the strengths in the other—their wisdom, their wit, their resilience, their courage, etc., we are more likely to surrender the demand that "we know better" and that others follow "what we know." What we find is a new sense of freedom and an abundant source of support.

My Way or the Highway

Determination or any of the values that fuel this "come from" are in fact helpful traits. However, if it happens to intercede with a belief that produces the stance "My way or the highway," the relational consequences will result in unwanted dynamics. The rigidity imposed and felt in this stance is overwhelming for all involved. The individual holding the belief faces frequent—if not constant—anxiety and stress, and the people involved report a sense of suffocation, a need to rebel or challenge the stance, and a loss of individuation. Vulnerability is key if this stance is to be abandoned. Said vulnerability will allow access to the values and the ability to re-route the opinion to a better functioning stance; one that not only supports the value but allows for mutual growth and contribution.

Keeping Score

There is an old adage that claims marriage is a 50/50 endeavor. For some strange reason many couples make every effort to function this way; a "quid pro quo" system that spans from finances to infidelity.

The truth is that marriage requires 100/100 and can not sustain tit for tat for long, not without harm to well-being.

As with the other common opinions, Keeping Score is anchored in "benevolent" values. This envelops the resulting behavior in a form of righteousness. This, in turn, produces a great deal of difficulty to recognize its harmful effects.

Keeping score is often heard in the couple's verbal exchanges: "You had an affair, why can't I?" Unfortunately, it is a more covert process, and uncovering it requires either brutal self-awareness or the assistance of a trained professional. Their task is to help unearth patterns, heal the broken dynamics, and put in place practices that assist the couple to learn a new way to relate.

Addressing Personal Opinions

No change takes place, not in a person or in a relationship, until we are in enough pain to make it happen. Addressing personal opinions will require the recognition of the need to change and the integration of a Self-Awareness Practice.

Self-Awareness: A Communication Mandate

We usually function from a position of being in control of ourselves, of knowing how we are coming across or how we are doing. But with little effort we can realize that we are often at the mercy of our opinions, our emotions, and our internal reactions and completely unaware of how they impact our behavior. Much like communication is not one-faceted, our internal world is a multifaceted and complicated landscape. Learning to be present and self-aware takes determination and ongoing effort. But that effort is worthwhile, since self-awareness is necessary in order to connect with another person in a real way. The most direct way to self-awareness is developing a Self-Inquiry Practice.

A Self-Inquiry Practice with the goal of self-awareness requires that our attention be directed inward on a regular basis. It includes creating a space or taking the time to scan our bodies and internal experience and NOTIC-ING what is present. All that is present must then be identified in words—pain, cold, sad… As obvious as this may sound, developing a vocabulary for what we experience can be a "tall order." We are highly trained to avoid our internal processes, so the words associated with emotional experiences may escape us. Add to the previously mentioned "tall order" putting words to psychological experiences, and the difficulty mounts.

A Self-Inquiry Practice can be understood as a mindfulness strategy with the goal of honing into our internal experience. Recognizing anything from physical pain to emotional irritability can help us effectively communicate what we need, what we are able to handle, and how much we can process. Recognizing where-we-are-at makes effective communication possible.

Refer to the Tools Section for recommended practices, additional resources and tools.

Increasing self-awareness is a goal onto itself, but its byproducts are exponentially beneficial. One of the most apparent is the heightened ability to clearly, honestly, even respectfully express ourselves. In the process of expression, we find deeper connection to self and others. Another by-product is enhanced ability to listen in curiosity, leaving aside judgment and the need to formulate a response. When we listen from curiosity, we experience greater intimacy, connection, understanding, and acceptance, as well as personal and relational growth.

Interpersonal Opinions

Couples create a shared culture based on mutually accepted opinions—the place where beliefs and values meet. These opinions expand from their view of themselves and each other to how they conjointly see the world. Interpersonal beliefs are the infrastructure of a couple's culture and can be spoken and unspoken as well as conscious or unconscious.

A rupture in the infrastructure occurs when a member of the couple abandons an agreed-upon belief without communicating the change to their partner. An undisclosed rupture of the infrastructure may ignite conflict or even cause the end of a relationship. Certainly we will not have access to the unconscious opinions, but the better our handle on the shared opinions, the better we will be at communicating any internal processes that may be morphing our individual stance.

Here is an example of a fracture in infrastructure:

Trevor & Alyssa

When they moved in together, Trevor and Alyssa agreed that they would maintain clear boundaries with extended family. Fifteen years into their relationship, Trevor had his mother stay over for a weekend—that lasted three weeks. When Alyssa asked how much longer "the guest's" visit would last, Trevor got angry and a disagreement ensued. Once in therapy, we discovered that as Trevor noticed his mother's aging, his belief on the need for boundaries from extended family changed. Because the change was not processed with Alyssa, the long visit became a challenge for the relationship.

Addressing Fractures in Interpersonal Opinions

We adopt practices such as exercise, avoiding icy sidewalks, not walking in the dark, or taking calcium supplements to prevent breaking a bone. Likewise, we need to practice effective communication to avoid the hardships caused by fractures in interpersonal opinions.

This is not to say that changes in opinions are undesirable. Much to the contrary, it is in the constant upgrading of ourselves and our opinions that we find growth. However, if a relationship is to succeed, our internal changes and struggles must be communicated openly, especially to our intimate partner.

Individuals in couples tend to buy into the idea that the other person can or should be able to read their mind, know what they feel or what they want—mind reading. Mind reading can be understood as resistance to openly declare our thinking on issues ranging from emotional needs to psychological struggles to sexual desires to what we want for dinner.

Being unadulterated in our self-expression is imperative to avoid or overcome relational fractures associated with interpersonal opinions.

Language

We've all seen the movies where a passionate, romantic relationship begins between two individuals from different parts of the world who only share the language of love. While that does happen, at some point the pair will choose a language to be learned and shared. This includes cultural dialects and slang. Sharing a birthplace or common language does not guarantee that the same words or phrases mean the same things. Any word can be interpreted differently.

Exercise: *When feasible, say the word ORANGE where many people can hear you. Ask as many as would tell you what they thought of when they heard the word. Here is what we've found: the word "orange", as all other words we commonly use, conjures up a different image for each person. Some think of the fruit, others of an orange fruit that is not an orange, other a sunset, others a shade of orange... it goes on and on. One simple word can mean so much!*

Most couples will naturally develop vocabularies with words they can rely on to have specific meanings. Still, taking the time—particularly during difficult or important conversations—to clarify meaning will go a long way. The simple act of curiously checking if what we hear is what they mean is likely to contribute to make conversations more effective and efficient.

To get through the task of inquiry, we must be committed to non-judgmentally ask for clarification in the moment. Additionally, we have to make an effort to show ongoing commitment to understand what words mean and how they are interpreted by one another from one conversation to the next. When clarification is needed, individuals can benefit from doing so in love with demonstrated patience. Judgmentally or dismissively approaching this process will hinder the relationship as a whole. The best approach is to be open and honest in the effort put forth to learn the meaning and the emotions behind the words.

Because language is a common occurrence, we take for granted that we must create a "together" linguistic style and vocabulary and that this is not a one-time effort. As we grow individually, so do the many ways we use and understand words. Staying curious and being interested in the other person are the right ingredients to sustain the needed attention.

In his outstanding book *Love Languages,* Gary D. Chapman assists couples to identify the way each member of the couple perceives they are loved. He identifies five Love Languages: *Physical Touch, Quality Time, Receiving Gifts, Acts of Service,* and *Words of Affirmation.* When individuals make a concerted effort to learn what communicates love to the other, an interesting transformation happens.

Body language

Studies show that, contrary to general belief, verbal communication only accounts for a fraction of what others interpret from us. A very high percentage of what and how we communicate is said through our body language. How we carry ourselves during an interaction with others delivers information that gets understood by complicated filters addressed above. Simplifying the signals we put out and being cognizant of how we come across can be a great catalyst to improving communication. For example, if a spouse is distracted (such as on a mobile device) while someone is trying to say something, they are likely to feel dismissed or uncared for. Likewise, looking at someone with interest and respect encourages discussion and trust. Displaying an intentional body language can help us create the kind of communication needed. Just by choosing the positioning of our body, the expression of our face, and gestures in our hands we contribute to a safe, inviting atmosphere for true emotions to be shared or an aggressive or undesirable environment.

The principles behind this way of behaving are consideration, mutual respect, valuing of the relationship, and a desire to cooperate or collaborate in the discussion or resolution of important issues.

Cultural and Gender Issues

We all make assumptions about how others communicate. Generalizations can be centered on birthplace, ethnicity, nationality, gender, sexual orientation... The list goes on and on.

Men and women have set assumptions about how the opposite sex communicates. While some generalizations are proven over time to be true, others don't hold up. Take, for example, the assumption that women only talk from their emotions and hold onto things too long or that men only talk about food, sports, and sex. While these assumptions are based on common and observable behavior, the truth is that men have access to emotions as much as women do and women are just as capable of talking about food, sports, and sex. By the way, when men are talking about food, sports, and sex, emotions are intensely present. Likewise, women can have pragmatic conversations where emotions are not considered. The moment any of us internally exclaims "There she goes again" or "There he goes again," we block our ability to listen, be present, and understand. Assumptions are not truth. Much like personal stances, assumptions blind us to the abundance of possibility present in each and every conversation—even when these are disagreements or arguments.

Because communication is distinctive from person to person, our focus is best placed in getting clear how we communicate first and how our intimate partner communicates second. Invest the time to learn each other's patterns, habits, and non-verbal cues and behaviors, and adapt when needed so communication flows.

We have worked with many couples who were of different cultural backgrounds. Part of the counseling experience for them has been to recognize that there is going to be a "moving learning curve" with respect to communication. Couples with different cultural backgrounds need to be conscious of all the points previously made at a higher level. Take, for example, what would be required for a woman from the Middle East and a man from the Southern United States to be in a successful couple-hood. There is no doubt that such a match can work, but they will need to enhance their efforts and employ all tools available to find satisfaction and fulfillment in their union.

Be curious, ask questions, seek understanding, but be respectful in every step. Learn about each other's culture, including which parts are negotiable and non-negotiable within an intimate relationship and in general. Ask how you can be supportive of their culture.

Family of Origin Impact

Underestimating the impact of the style we adopted from our family of origin can get us in sticky situations. It bears remembering that we were highly influenced by many factors as we developed into who we are and how we communicate and relate to others. Some of the influencing factors include where we grew up, the way we were raised, the communicational dynamics among the adults around us, and the way people addressed each other and us during that time.

We learned how to communicate and how to relate from our family of origin. Good or bad, we are products of that environment. Many learned that screaming and name-calling was the way to communicate, where others learned that self-expression is not acceptable.

Because we were molded over time, addressing family of origin impact is also a process that happens over time. Acknowledging our communication's background is a step in the right direction. Abandoning any ideas that our background is of greater worth or somehow better than our partner's will further the path to closeness.

Cathy & Elmer   *Cathy and Elmer were from the same country. Elmer's family (two sisters and two brothers) had moved to the United States when he was five years old. Cathy's mom and dad presented as happy and she reports never seeing them fight. Elmer moved to the same city six years later at the age of 16. His father never married his mother and had many relationships that Elmer was exposed to. When Cathy and Elmer met, he was married but did not disclose this fact. Their relationship was in the 10th month when they entered treatment. Cathy had recently discovered that he was married. She reported: "He was unfaithful a few times, but I thought, hey, if I am patient and show him I love him, he will change… Little did I know he was cheating on his wife with me!" When Elmer was asked what he wanted out of therapy, he stated: "I grew up with cheating as a way of life—what men do. But now I am ready to leave my marriage. I want to change my ways and have things work with Cathy."*

When the issues causing discord in a couple are related to their family history or cultural differences, individual work—therapy—can benefit the individuals and the couple. Behaving as if the issues will self-resolve is a dangerous delusion and, ultimately, a waste of time for all involved.

There are two communication patterns commonly learned in the family of origin: *fear of rejection* and *emotionality*. *Fear of rejection* can be crippling. It prevents the person who feels it from making requests or speaking their mind. It has a cause-and-effect pattern that has confirmed for the person that when they speak up love, acceptance, compassion and a long slew of other much-needed responses will be withheld. *Emotionality* or an insistent reliance on what is felt as the source of all truth and reality is also crippling. When an individual is unable to separate feeling from reason, they experience a sense of being overwhelmed. Frequent responses to this state include shutdown, desperate crying, anxiety, and depressive symptoms.

Secrets to Effective Intimate Communication

Here's the scoop: The secrets will depend on our current pitfalls, so rather than assuming that the following is a comprehensive list or that the suggestions will work for everyone would be misleading.

The phrase *Effective Intimate Relationships* is defined as a space where all involved are fully self-expressed. Where that expression is revered and encouraged and vulnerability is rewarded with equal openness and honesty.

There are some characteristics that can be expected in effective intimate relationships and, consequently, their communication style. These include:
- *Trust*—Both partners insist that the other's safety is paramount and take the needed measures to ensure it
- *Openness*—about who we are and what we want
- *Acceptance*—without judgment

- *Respect*—holding the other in the highest regard
- *Encouraged*—build each other up, provide hope, and motivate
- *Genuine*—be sincere and authentic where each person's uniqueness can thrive
- *Honesty*—tell the truth, always
- *Curiosity*—inquire and question your loved one as if there is nothing known
- *Vulnerability*—be open, choose courage to be real
- *Perseverance*—show commitment and determination
- *Celebrate progress and mutual success*—focus on the positive
- *Gratitude*—acknowledging the gifts to foster tender moments
- *Humility*—toward self and the other. In humility we accept ourselves and each other for who we truly are, not who we want each other to be; humility will allow us the opportunity to look at life through someone else's eyes.

There may be other important characteristics. As those show up, share them, explain them, and position them as opportunities for growth. By doing this fear of intimacy is reduced and trust increased.

John & Traci

John and Traci married while both were in their late 30's; John for the second time, Traci for the first. They had met at church and, therefore, had some things in common like their faith, political views, and certain hobbies. They dated for six months before becoming engaged.

During pre-marital counseling, both revealed that there were certain aspects of their sexual history that they felt important to share with each other. However, they feared how the other would respond. We were able to discuss the expectations and needs each had regarding communication and set the foundation on which anything could be shared. John and Traci were able to share their past in a non-threatening manner and both reported how much closer they felt after "the truth" was spoken.

Putting this all together

We have discussed barriers and expectations regarding communication; but while knowledge is good, practice is key.

Listening

There is more to communication than the words we say. Being an engaged listener is the first step in building a deeper, stronger intimate relationship. Listening is a skill that requires ongoing practice. There are qualities that enhance the listening:

- Pay Attention
- Avoid Judgment and Criticism
- Provide Feedback
- Be Consistent

Pay Attention

Distraction is a deterrent to communication. When in conversation, our focus needs to be on achieving a goal that will support the relationship as well as the individuals in it. When our mind is wandering or pulled by different issues at the same time, important parts fall by the way and are missed. Reading a text while a spouse is speaking may allow us to hear the words, but will we notice the tone of voice they are using? Their body language? The look of their face? Or whether or not they are making eye contact? Making an effort to converse while face-to-face; mindful that the body is relaxed and comfortable, not tense and closed; eye contact should be consistent so as to avoid distractions. Being mindful of these small details will have a huge impact on the quality of the communication. Look in the *Resources & Tools* Chapter for the LALAS tool. This will increase listening skill.

Avoid Judgment and Criticism

Withholding judgment and criticism is a practice that involves self-control and the ability to move away from our personal perspective. By removing them, freedom of expression and the ability to trust ensue. The goal in conversation is learning and understanding, not blaming or winning. To learn, we must be open to new information found in old words.

Provide feedback

In this skill we demonstrate our level of listening. We do so by summarizing what is heard. It is not required that we mirror what we hear word for word, but that we state what we understood. Doing so while asking for further clarifications if needed will enhance the process.

Communicating effectively is not a talent we are born with, nor a skill acquired overnight. It requires purpose, practice, commitment and constant review and upgrade of what is known.

Reader's Thoughts

What does it feel like when you are listened to?

What is it like to fully get what another person is saying?

chapter nine

Spiritual Perspectives

Regardless of the traditions or religions followed, the spiritual realm is a foundational space that must be tapped any time effort is exerted towards a growth-promoting goal. Improving our intimate relationships qualify as such a goal.

Religious writings from all faiths and philosophies provide a great deal of guidance regarding how we should interact with each other. The teachings found in spiritual books provide instructions regarding how to love, respect, communicate, and support. These teachings can be used to encourage, instruct, and provide trusted reminders of how we are to live and love.

> We differentiate between spirituality and religiosity.
> Additionally, we encourage spirituality as defined
> by the individuals themselves. To us, the major
> distinction in spirituality is the experience of awe.
> We believe that awe-inspiring moments, shared
> regularly will enhance a couple's connection.

Christians and non-Christians insist on the constant and committed effort to self-growth and improvement. All point to principles intended to shape and develop character traits meant to bring forth a sense of satisfaction throughout life and, very specifically, at life's end. Without attribution to any religion or tradition, the instructions on developing character include:

Behavioral Standards

Some examples of behavioral standards include honesty, transparency, sincerity, loyalty, and integrity—to name a few. From a therapeutic perspective, keeping behavioral standards enhances self-esteem, provides a foundation for growth, and allows for uninhibited personal connections as well as the removal or prevention of regret.

Service

Provide loving service for the sake of serving as opposed to a way of securing a desired outcome or reward. Research confirms that service engenders kind feelings and even love, not just in the receiver, but the person doing the service. When partners serve each other, they are in fact enhancing their own feelings towards the other. The task here is to seek opportunities to serve together and serve each other and do so without expectation of something in return.

Gratitude

Gratitude gives way to acknowledging how others—including a higher power—contribute to our lives. It has been linked to a sense of well-being and connection. When we are at our emotional best, we are more likely to treat others with kindness and respect. Similarly, when we feel connected, we are more likely to be honest and open with each other. To be clear, this is not about having a grateful attitude. This is the intentional practice of gratitude, which may include:

- A gratitude journal
- Formal acknowledgement of things, behaviors, acts, etc. we are grateful for and express gratitude about via cards, calls, text and social media posts
- Daily outward thanks to each other—not in passing but on purpose

Be devoted to your life partner and keep the relationship alive by making it a priority. Faithfulness, kindness, loyalty, and gentleness are spiritual characteristics that unfurl to majestic daily practices and contribute richly to the development of closeness in our most important relationships. Many religions encourage family time and time for the couple to spend alone. Date night is not to be reserved for the courting phase of the relationship, but must be a practice carried out perpetually.

Shared Spiritual Practice

Develop practices that nurture spiritual bonds. This includes religious rituals but expands beyond that to include practices that the couple recognizes as linkages to each other and that which is larger than themselves. Couples report that simple things such as:

- Taking walks in silence
- Visiting places that cause awe
- Meditating together—don't just talk about it but come together to "be" as opposed to "do"
- Praying together—whatever shape prayer takes for you pray together and for each other. Do so about the little things and the big things
- Reading books together. Choose books that ignite conversations and assist exploration

Support each other in spiritual pursuits and share the satisfaction felt in that pursuit. This endeavor will enhance closeness and insight.

Sex as a Spiritual Practice

Develop a satisfying sexual life. It may seem strange that we are including sexual intimacy under the spiritual section of this book. But in our eyes, there is no better placing. The vulnerability required for sexual intimacy makes this topic or area of life a close parallel to spiritual experience. Additionally, a satisfying sexual life can have transcendental effects to the individuals and the relationship. It is also apropos that we cover this topic in this chapter, as sexual needs, appetites, and desires left undisclosed can in fact have a devastating effect on the individuals and the couples they are part of.

Jack & Sondra

Jack had been married to Sondra for over 20 years. He never disclosed his deepest sexual desires. Left unfulfilled and even ashamed, he chose to fill those desires outside of the marriage with the devastating results of destroying his marital relationship, deeply hurting all members of his family and his community.

In absolute contrast, the following story shows the potential benefits of opening up and seeking sexual satisfaction within intimate relationships.

Jim and his wife, Nancy, had been married over 15 years when he entered therapy. Jim brought up his issues, which included an intense need for new sexual experiences, a recent opportunity to accomplish his desires outside of the marriage, and his torment about staying faithful to his wife.

Jim & Nancy

We discussed the difficulties in communicating his wishes to his wife and found that culture, faith, the sexual practices they were used to as well as his own judgment about his desires got in the way. In time, Jim invited Nancy to therapy, and a series of healing and building sessions began. The couple took up the challenge of researching together what could fit in their sexual repertoire. They committed to withhold judgment and talk through any perceived hang-ups. Lastly, they agreed to recognize and honor their sexual interactions as a tool to get closer to each other.

Overcoming sexual inhibitions, honoring sexual needs, and having the willingness to experiment and try new things will, in fact, serve as foundation and support to a blooming relationship and will enhance the spiritual connection for the couple.

Forgiveness and Surrender

Practice forgiveness and surrender. These are exquisite spiritual efforts that keep us in the present moment as opposed to the past.

Forgiveness refers to letting go of the hurts and disappointments. It includes:

- Relinquishing the need to hold others as our debtors
- Seeing others as more than their mistakes
- Finding empathy towards others as we integrate the fact that we, too, can make mistakes that can cause others pain and hurt
- Giving up on the insistence that the other person should have known better

Surrender refers to an emotional state where we don't insist that "things" must be as we think they should but lean into and accept the way they are. A surrendered stance includes:

- Buying into the idea that what is happening is not happening to ME, simply happening
- Accepting that we are equipped to manage the situations, challenges, and difficulties or have the capacity to secure help as needed
- Releasing conditions to happiness or joy. Too many of us are committed to the idea that when X happens then I'll be happy. Surrendering these beliefs and the rigidity associated with them will surely improve mood, mental capacity will increase, and internal peace will be accessed
- Face the possibility that we have become addicted to drama and hysteria and resolve to give those up for better coping skills

Spiritual awareness, development, and practice are foundational to individual betterment. No couple can improve their relationship without improving individuals first; and no individual can improve him- or herself without addressing spirituality. In our extensive experience working with couples within different spiritual and religious paradigms, we have learned that when couples work on developing a shared spiritual practice, their relationship deepens and the qualities that make the relationship fulfilling and enjoyable are enhanced.

Annie & Jamie

When Annie and Jamie met they did not share a spiritual foundation, and seven years into their marriage they are as different as they can be in this regard. Yet they have developed traditions and behaviors that support their spiritual development and enhance their relationship. Jamie is not a Christian, but he attends services regularly. When unable to do so he makes it possible for Annie to attend. Additionally, they have created holidays and family traditions that allow for both cultures and beliefs to be honored. They share awe-inspiring moments on purpose and give them words so the other person can understand the experience from their perspective. When they faced cancer and infertility, the therapeutic work was supported by their spiritual experiences. Listening to them helped us understand that love, dedication and effort can bridge the deepest of gaps.

Reader's Thoughts

If spirituality was a set of chosen practices,
what would you choose to include?

How would you invite your significant other
to help choose and contribute to the chosen
practice(s)?

chapter ten

Power of Reconciliation

Y ou had another fight, one of you said you are sorry, but you've seen this so many times before that you know it won't last.

"Things will be better for a little bit, but soon the same habits and behaviors will return and we'll be right back in this same place."

"My faith tells me that I should forgive, and in my heart I know that forgiveness heals the relationship, but I'm also tired of being taken advantage and staying on this hamster wheel...it's a pattern that just does not change!"

"I can't help but think that maybe I'm doing something wrong since we stay in this rut and I don't like the way I feel towards them but I'm just not sure what to do anymore."

Arguments, fights, and disagreements are going to happen in any relationship. Pride, false assumptions, anger, and bitterness all lead to conflict. One of the best ways to overcome intimate compassion fatigue in your relationship is being able to forgive and reconcile, but what does this actually mean? We hear the terms, but it has been our experience that many think of forgiveness as "I must accept what happened, forget about it and move on as if nothing happened." This is not our proposed path.

Forgiveness is the intentional act you take to change your feelings, attitudes, and actions about what happened. Instead of harboring ongoing negative attitudes towards the individual or situation, there is a focus on the offender's well-being. Hoping that whatever hurt or wrong they have caused you will lead them to consider their actions and make permanent changes. There is nothing wrong with hoping that they will become respectful, loving, and caring, but forgiveness is letting go of the hurt you feel inside. It is not something we do for them. We forgive for our sake, our well-being, and our growth.

However, forgiveness does not always lead to reconciliation of the relationship. Reconciliation is our coming back together following a hurt, argument, or disagreement; to be perfectly honest, there are many times when forgiveness occurs but reconciliation should not, such as in the case of abuse. But when the goal is to reconcile, all must realize that it is a process. There is not nor ever will be an expectation that just because you have been forgiven, all is well and there will be a return to the way things were. Reconciliation takes time. While forgiveness focuses on the attitude and behavior of the one wronged, reconciliation focuses on the attitudes and actions of the offender. For example, just because you say you are sorry for what happened, I may not necessarily believe you until I see a change. People are very good at saying what you want to hear, but real change comes in their actions over time—especially when there is a history of saying the right things but doing the wrong.

Reconciliation is about trust: can I trust that you will do and say the right things that will not cause me harm? The foundation of any loving, caring relation is trust. When that trust is broken once or repeatedly the only thing that restores it is time. Words by themselves will not restore trust; it will take seeing changes in actions. Trusting again is a process that takes time, and any setbacks or return to previous behaviors will delay the process. As trust is being re-established, remember that there are certain factors that play into the timing of reconciliation, including: history of the behavior; depth of the betrayal; level of sincerity versus superficial acts; and the genuine attitude of the offender.

How do you know that someone is genuine when it comes to their desire to reconcile? Steve Cornell, in his article *How to Move from Forgiveness to Reconciliation*, lists seven signs that display true repentance.

1. Accepts full responsibility for his or her actions. (Instead of: "Since you think I've done something wrong..." or "If I have done anything to offend you...")
2. Welcomes accountability from others.
3. Does not continue in the hurtful behavior or anything associated with it.
4. Does not have a defensive attitude about being in the wrong.
5. Does not dismiss or downplay the hurtful behavior.
6. Does not resent doubts about their sincerity or the need to demonstrate sincerity—especially in cases involving repeated offenses.
7. Makes restitution where necessary.

If the individual is not displaying these actions, then their actions are most likely not sincere. However, if the individual is making an effort and demonstrating their desire to reconcile the relationship with you, it is important to know whether you are being receptive. If there is hesitancy on your part, Mr. Cornell mentions a few factors for you to be aware of, including: being aware of your motives; being in prayer for the one who hurt you; considering any of your own actions that might have contributed to the problem; being honest about your feelings and need for time with the other person; stating clearly what you are expecting to see as a change in their behavior; and being realistic about the process and expectations.

Just because there may be forgiveness and reconciliation does not mean that there are not consequences. Our actions and words might be forgiven by the person offended and reconciliation can occur in many instances but we may still be left with emotional consequences like feelings of guilt, hurt, fear, resentment, sorrow, pain, embarrassment and our reputation tainted. There may be physical impact such as injury, disease, depression, anxiety, loss of sleep and impact on our energy level. We might lose our job, finances, home and economic stability. Sometimes our consequences include separation from more than just our significant other as we might lose friends and other family members.

While we may not be able to escape the consequences of our behaviors it does not mean that we should not attempt to reconcile the relationship. When we truly realize that the relationship is more important than whatever the issue was we will do whatever we need to reconcile. We remember that love conquers all things, hopes all things and never fails. With that mindset forgiveness and reconciliation can happen.

Reader's Thoughts

How would you describe successful reconciliation?

chapter eleven

Resources & Tools

Most of us have toolboxes in our homes and in them we have hammers, screwdrivers, wrenches, etc. Even so, surely I am not the only person who has tried to bang a nail in a wall with a shoe heel, or insisted that a knife would do the job of taking out a screw. My personal excuse for trying these rudimentary ways of completing simple tasks is kind of telling—I give in to the idea that the shoe is easily accessible and taking the time to go get the hammer just makes the task more time-consuming and complicated. In some ways, my thinking may be right... it is easier to use the shoe... but does the shoe complete the job properly? The answer is "no." Most of the time the shoe is by far not the right tool.

If this has not happened to you, then my face is blushing as I confess that way too often I end up spending much more time and effort cleaning up the shoe-marked wall, going to the basement to first find the tool box and then retrieve the hammer... not to mention the complications of having to schedule time and arrange my budget to go get another pair of shoes.

Here's my point: there may be other ways to get tasks completed, but tools, when actually used as they are meant to, will no doubt do a better job than their many possible substitutions.

Having the tools in the box does not make the job easier. We have to determine that we will actually use the right tools for the right jobs. We have to commit to spending time learning to use the tools and invest in acquiring more tools as needed.

The following tools can make the challenge of managing a Hijacked Brain better, but they will have no effect if left inside this book. They have to be used, shared, practiced, reviewed, applied, and adapted to your own experience and needs. Discussing these tools openly and partnering together will enhance your relationships.

As a reminder:

The Hijacked Brain is defined as a period of time (moments, hours or days) when an individual feels carried away by emotions and is unable to feel in control of reactions and thoughts. While this experience can run the gamut from mild to severe, all who are affected report disruptions in the management of life with clear consequences to their most precious relationships.

First Tool: A cheat sheet to get you on your way:

1. Pay attention to each other and prioritize your relationship above all else. Remember that where you put your attention is where you put your heart.

2. Keep your individuality sacred. Don't forget that your relationship exists because *YOU* exist and matter—nurture yourself and your interests and support your partner to do the same.

3. Argue with passion but do it to *LEARN*, not to win. The need to win is a selfish impulse. An intent to learn will bring you closer and make your union stronger.

4. Stay curious about each other. Never assume you *KNOW* your partner and stay willing to grow together even if sometimes that means growing a little apart.

5. Create community. First between the two of you—make that a solid union and then serve and allow yourselves to be served by others. Your life will be enriched by the ripples made in the community you belong to and make a difference in.

6. Remember that falling in love is less important than *STAYING* in love; and staying in love has little to do with love and everything to do with *LOYALTY, HONESTY, DEDICATION, COOPERATION* and *COMMITMENT.* These are behaviors, not feelings. Behavior is a choice, not something that happens by chance.

7. Laugh. Don't take yourself, your partner or what is happening too seriously. Find ways to laugh and make each other laugh. Do that on purpose.

8. Create memories by being present in your life. Don't allow yourself to ever function out of habit—Be *PRESENT.* It is the best gift you can give yourself, each other and the world.

9. Look for the good things in each other. Even when you are angry, make yourself remember what is good instead of focusing on what is wrong.

10. In whatever way you can or want, *SHARE* a spiritual practice so that *GOD—A HIGHER POWER—SOURCE—PURE ENERGY* can be a part of your life experience and a refuge you can go to *ALWAYS.* Make gratitude part of that spiritual practice. Know that all you have, do or are has been given to you, so your best move is to be *THANKFUL.*

Charting the dynamic

The next tool is intended to help identify patterns. This step is essential, as it assists self observation, introspection, taking personal responsibility and acknowledging your contribution to the dynamics.

Learn your rhythm:

When people commit to a therapeutic relationship, the therapist has the luxury of noticing patterns LIVE. In my practice, I do not point out a pattern until I've seen it or noticed it at least three times. Since waiting to see patterns myself can take a while, I engage my clients in my investigative process. Clients are to keep a record of their mood by marking a calendar daily with an indication of the type of day they had:

Good Day	Anxious Day	Energized Day	Depressed Day	Angry Day	A little of everything Day

A good day is characterized by managed behavior. Even if mood was altered by an event, the individual is reporting an ability to choose their reaction, as opposed to being at the mercy of their reactions.

Anxious days include experiences such as "Butterflies in the stomach," any degree of paranoia, uneasiness, and/or suspicion. Anxious days can be mild or severe and are clearly differentiated from an energized day by a sense of dread and the need or insistence that "the other shoe will drop any minute now."

On **energized days**, people feel capable of accomplishing any and all tasks. They seem to be on a full tank of fuel. If tiredness does approach, a quick nap or a moment of retreat is all that is need to keep at it. There can be a focused intent to get one project completed or a bit of ADHD as many tasks are being worked on at the same time. Regardless of your energy style, these days seem to be very productive, with some anxiety over completion, but more clearly described by desire and excitement.

Not difficult to describe, the **depressed day** finds the individual having difficulty to address—let alone complete—tasks. Even in high-functioning individuals, depressed days slow people down and include sadness, sometimes irritability, negative thinking, and a pervasive sense of gloom. Depressed days can also vary in intensity and duration. Their sad effect can include regret, confusion, and more sadness.

The **angry, irritable days** can be accompanied by some degree of energy, but is it usually characterized by some sense of having your rights, space, or ideas diminished or disrespected. This may be one of the most difficult types of days to distinguish, as it also has some sadness and negative thinking in the mix.

The major characteristic of this type of day is the pervasive intent to argue. Reason or correctness is irrelevant. The energy sees only one way to work itself out, and that is in active disagreement with anyone who will enter the dynamic.

This type of day needs little to be understood. It contains many—if not all—of the states mentioned before and may even create some unexpected ones.

A little of everything days are the most exhausting ones for all involved because they bring about extreme effort to manage an inexplicably changing behavioral landscape. The person experiencing it may be as confused as those in relationship with them. Depending on the intensity of the experience, this type usually prepares the way for a difficult next day.

The calendar is marked for a few months and the patterns begin to emerge on their own. This exercise proves beneficial even by individuals and couples who do not discover well-marked patterns. The reason is that the process or practice of paying attention, also known as mindfulness, and a separate tool on its own affords them a wealth of information that enriches access to themselves and each other. This tool, the "Learn your rhythm" tool, unearths dynamics often hidden from the naked eye.

**Annie &
Jamie**

Annie and Jamie came to therapy in the seventh year of their relationship. By then, they had been married for five years, living together for one and the proud parents of two children, ages four and two. They agree that their relationship has had its ups and downs but recently they are both very reactive, making the lows deeper and longer in duration. Annie says that sometimes Jamie just explodes and she is left wondering what is happening. Jamie reports that he is not always aware of what causes his "tantrums," but that he does noticed them, after the fact. After three sessions, we all agreed that looking at their rhythms may be interesting. We continued meeting weekly, often spending some time dissecting the experience of introspection required to complete the calendar. We also integrated other tools to be discussed later in the chapter and looked at progress in their shared dynamic.

Jumping three months later, we observed a number of things:

Annie had always experienced mood swings around the time she was due to get her period. Nine years ago, when they began their committed relationship, Jamie would make light of the situation and Annie worked hard to suppress her reactions. However, about six months before coming to therapy, Annie was less inclined to suppress or control her reactions. Annie credited new stressors at work as the cause of her inability to manage her reactions. She became increasingly gloomy and irritable, finding fault in just about everything Jamie did or said. Jamie perceived her moods and reactions as criticism and rejection.

Jamie tried to use old coping mechanisms, including humor and light-hearted responses, but those were not received well, often deepening Annie's mood. They observed that Jamie's explosions began two months before coming to therapy and were still in full force in the months we were recording their rhythms. They also observed that the explosions would emerge three to four days before Annie's "monthly depression" began. Jamie had effectively found a way to distance himself from Annie and avoid the hurt he experienced during her depressive days. However, Annie perceived his explosions as abandonment.

Now, it is important to note that none of this behavior was conscious. Annie was not purposefully feeling sad and picking on Jamie. And Jamie was not looking for a way to protect himself. They were acting or being acted upon by hormonally-induced moods. Both of them were affected. While Jamie can say that his estrogen did not play a part in this, we can clearly see that his cortisol was heightened by the perceived threat of the upcoming PMS.

Couples engage in dynamics that do not serve them. Getting out of those dynamics requires conscious effort, purposeful attention, and mutual cooperation.

Recognize your Triggers

Triggers? Yes, triggers. Too often partners' slightest tilt of the head, roll of the eye, or grimace becomes the reason for an argument. Hormonal changes in women, or the suspicion of hormonal change by a partner, can heighten not just what is noticed, but also the meaning attributed to what we see.

In recognizing triggers, a person owns the behaviors that bring about reactions, but once triggers are identified, meaning must be abandoned. The person triggered is now responsible to name the trigger, access their own vulnerability, and register how they feel, communicate the feeling and stay open to either correction, or accepting/negotiating their partner's position.

One BIG human behavior truth is that we have been taught that we have a right to our emotions. True. But we do not have a right to our assumptions, nor to the full scale of available reactions. Triggers will happen. But they are topics of conversation, not excuses for impositions or demands.

Hugging a Porcupine: Touch

In his masterful book, *How to Hug a Porcupine—Dealing With Toxic & Difficult to Love Personalities*, Dr. John Lewis Lund goes into detail about how to connect with people with personality disorders. While this topic is outside the scope of this book, the visual presented by the title serves to describe what it can feel like to connect to each other during hormonally-induced mood changes. Partners can become so rigid during this time, that isolation and feelings of abandonment can ensue.

The tool being proposed here is touch. Positive psychology and other disciplines are focusing on the role of cortisol and oxytocin in human connections. Judith Glasser, behavioral anthropologist and author of *Conversational Intelligence*, presented the following definitions:

Cortisol is one of several steroid hormones produced by the adrenal cortex, and which acts as a neurotransmitter in the brain, whose levels in the blood may become elevated in response to physical or psychological stress. In [conversation], cortisol is released in [moments] of distrust, and activates protective behavior.

Oxytocin is a feel good hormone produced by the pituitary gland and acts as a neurotransmitter in the brain. It produces feelings of connection or close bond. Oxytocin is released in [moments] of trust and promotes connectivity.

Unlike estrogen and progesterone, which are mainly female hormones,, cortisol and oxytocin are human hormones and found in both men and women.

Why all the talk about cortisol and oxytocin? Because we can manipulate their levels in each other and ourselves. Touch, the tool we are discussing, increases oxytocin (also known as the cuddle hormone).

Partners working to improve their relationship and overcome the consequences of hormonally-induced mood swings must pay attention to their physical connection during these times. Hold hands, massage shoulders, assist in the bathing process, hug, cuddle. Look for opportunities to increase oxytocin in each other and notice how that ameliorates discord.

An important note to the RIGID partner: all these tools, but touch in particular, require that you surrender beliefs, opinions, stances, insistence in your point of view and any other tool you utilize to support your rigidity. Both partners, but you in particular, must practice trust (more on that to come). You must practice melting into your partner's touch and allowing a feeling of closeness to emerge. This takes practice, and your partner will learn ways of assist in your releasing of the maladaptive tools. But you must be willing to surrender your weapons of war, be open to a new way of addressing your emotional needs and accept help to get it done.

Weapons of War

If we think carefully and honestly about it, we have go-to behaviors (a look, a verbal expression, a flip of the hand), something we do when we want to make others insignificant.

C'mon, you see it, right?

Take Trevor and Alyssa as an example:

Trevor had been doing something that really got under Alyssa's skin, rather than coming to him and addressing the issue, she rolled her eyes and said something about it while walking away. The combination of flippant and dismissive made Trevor feel very small—but that did not last. He lashed at her and screamed that he would not be treated like a child in his own home and if she had something to say she should come and say it to his face.

Trevor & Alyssa

Alyssa's weapon of war may not be loud and demanding, but they are effective in causing Trevor to feel "less-than" and that is never a relationship-nurturing state. On the other hand, Trevor's weapons of war are evident; anger and threatening behavior are just as effective at pushing Alyssa away.

Weapons of war are words, mannerisms, body language or any other behavior employed with the purpose of separating ourselves from others and doing so by creating a sense of inferiority, insignificance or disregard in them.

Regardless of the weapon used, if relationships are to be repaired, improved, nurtured, and made so that we want to be in them, weapons must be buried, abandoned, exchanged for tools to build rather than destroy.

During a discussion about burying weapons of war, many people will ask the question: "How do I do that? I roll my eyes so automatically I don't think I would have time to stop myself!" We have come to believe that un-handing a weapon of war is only possible when:

- The well-being of the other person is a priority
- Being right is less important than understanding
- There is clarity about the pending needs
- There is willingness to be open, honest, and genuine
- Listening is as important as talking
- Learning is more important than reaching an agreement
- Trust is present

Creating a Culture of Trust as a Tool

One of the most impactful conversations I ever had happened early in my career. The conversation was between myself and my then-supervisor whom I will call Stephany. I was adamantly stating that she was forging a culture of distrust among the staff, to which she replied: "Trust is overrated." She had brilliantly brought me to a no-words state (a difficult task, I assure you). I left her office with a head full of thoughts and resigned my position a few weeks later.

Now, the story illustrates a few things:
- Words don't mean the same things to everyone
- Words always make a difference—you just can't predict what the difference will be
- If we don't agree on a definition of trust, there is no way to have a relationship

---

Trust is therefore defined as our ability to predict, with some degree of reliability, the constancy of another's behavior.

Driving is the best way to illustrate this. When we drive, even if we are defensive drivers, we are pretty confident that we will make it to our destination. We *TRUST* that the roads will be in good condition, that other drivers will stop and move as allowed by traffic lights and signs, and that our car will function as it is supposed to. Should we have *ANY* doubts about any of those points, we would alter our course. But we trust those things will be present, so we confidently get behind the wheel.

In relationships, effort must be exerted to promote a culture of trust, meaning that we will behave in accord with all that has been agreed *OR* we will discuss that with which we cannot follow through.

When Carmen and Ralf met, they both believed in open sexual relationships. They supported each other in that way of thinking until one day 15 years into their marriage, when Ralf said to Carmen he no longer wanted the same arrangement. This became a pivot point in their relationship and trust had to be redefined.

Carmen & Ralf

Trust is imperative. It is a priority—how it is shaped is less important than that there is agreement as to how it is experienced in the relationship.

To forge a culture of trust:

- Honesty must be encouraged and rewarded
- A change in perspective or belief must be met by curiosity
- Judgement is avoided
- Expectations are held as invitations, *NOT* conditions

If trust is an issue, repairing this area is more important than anything else. However, trust cannot be repaired on its own. It needs communication, attention, tenderness, conflict or disagreement, negotiation, clarification, willingness, support etc., etc., etc.

Making Each Fight its Own

Ninety percent of fights are not about what just happened, but an effort to resolve old disagreements. Curiously enough, arguments cannot be resolved in that format; in fact, by engaging in that behavior, couples perpetuate feelings of resentment.

Because so many people come to therapy to resolve conflict in their intimate relationships, a major therapeutic goal is to help couple have effective fights.

Effective fights are events when the parties passionately articulate their thoughts, opinions, desires and/or displeasure. They do so in full respect of the other person in the discussion. Their goal is to learn, understand, explain, explore. Resistance and unwillingness to participate will prove to harm the relationship.

Specifically, it will affect trust as a decline to participate is equaled to repelling an opportunity to allow individuals to be fully expressed. The hope is that members of a couple feel fully expressed and fully accepted. Effective fights are not an effort to prove someone right or wrong.

Self-Respect and Self Denial

Little can be accomplished without striking a balance between self-respect and self denial. Self-respect is achieved when we give our word and have the ability to take a stance that makes our priorities understood. Priorities and the non-negotiables we believe we can not do without. Self-denial requires an ability to suspend our non-negotiables for the sake of the relationship—not as in giving them up, but as in being open to amending them. An example may help:

Dori and José had one child and Dori wanted one more. José had an older child from a previous relationship, and did not want any more. José wanted new sexual experiences that were not of interest to Dori. They were both unwilling to discuss either issue. Their position was that a discussion could only lead to one of them having to give up or give into. What they learned is that in an open discussion— one meant to have them learn about the other rather than come to final decisions—created a new level of trust. They both had to get clear on their non-negotiables, find ways to express them and stay open, even hopeful, to gain insight about their partner through the conversation.

Dori & José

Intimate Compassion Fatigue Tool

Assessment

Now that you have read about intimate compassion fatigue, the following tool is designed to provide more insight for you as to whether you might be experiencing fatigue in your intimate relationship. This is not a scientific assessment to provide you a diagnosis, but instead is intended to help you see and understand your reactions in the relationship.

1 = None of the time   2 = Some of the time   3 = Most of the time

____ 1) You are preoccupied with uneasy feelings about your intimate partner/relationship.

____ 2) More often than not, you are apprehensive about spending time with your intimate partner.

____ 3) All details of the intimate relationship have left you feeling physically tired.

____ 4) Others see you acting different than normal.

____ 5) You have come to feel hopeless that your intimate relationship will improve.

____ 6) You feel blamed by your intimate partner for the problems in the relationship.

____ 7) You feel disappointed in the way you both act and talk to each other.

____ 8) Little things annoy you that did not in the past.

____ 9) You experience difficulty sleeping because of preoccupation with your intimate relationship.

____ 10) It's difficult to have fun together because you are not sure what kind of "mood" your intimate partner will show.

This is the type of assessment that you definitely want to have a 10! If this is your score, then congratulations! The intimate relationship is in a very good place and you should definitely keep up the great work.

If your score is 11 to 14, you may not have intimate compassion fatigue, but there are some warning signs to which you should be paying attention. Be aware of your reactions and take this assessment again on a monthly basis to monitor your scores.

After adding up your responses, if your score is higher than 15, you may be experiencing intimate compassion fatigue and it is time to access additional resources.

Getting Clear

What we call getting clear may be named self-awareness. Sometimes we know we are not happy or satisfied, but cannot conceive what is missing. Getting clear with ourselves is a requirement to getting clear with our partner.

Getting Clear Worksheet

How do you experience love?

What makes you feel connected?

How do you know that you are invested in a conversation?

Can you tell when you are faking interest/ happiness/connection?

If this is as good as it gets, is it enough?

Dynamics

The answers to this assessment will give you an idea of your relationship's strengths and weaknesses and guide your reading.

Dynamics Worksheet

Small disagreements frequently turn into unmanageable fights	Y	N
We have a language of our own	Y	N
Winning is individually important	Y	N
We often forget or block out the "good" in each other	Y	N
We prioritize our relationship	Y	N
We don't seem to exist outside of the relationship	Y	N
We fight effectively	Y	N
We maintain a high level of curiosity about each other	Y	N
We make efforts to be romantic and thoughtful	Y	N
We laugh together	Y	N

Body Language and Tone Assessment Tool

Self-awareness is our go-to tool to assess the way we contribute to a given dynamic. Practicing self-awareness is a matter of introspection. Consider this short assessment to assess your body language:

Body Language & Tone Assessment

Am I distracted or do I appear distracted?

Is my posture closed or open?

How can I position my self so that he/she knows I am interested?

Am I tense?

Can I relax?

Is the tone in my questions directing the discussion towards exploration or accusation?

By taking personal responsibility for the way we appear when in communication with others, we manage to minimize discord. We all want to be listened to; most of us will say that for the most part we don't need to be given what we want right now, what we need is to know is that our needs are being considered and that time and attention will be paid to the issues we want to bring up. When that time comes, we want all involved to be and to appear to be invested in working together for the benefit of all.

LALAS

Becoming self-aware while making progress in our ability to communicate in our intimate relationships can be a difficult task. To simplify reaching this goal, we suggest the following conversational tool: Listen, Ask, Listen Again, Share (LALAS).

Listen

We define listening as the act of being present and non-judgmentally paying attention to what is being said. It is not a time to prepare the opposing argument. True listening requires a deep sense of interest—not just in what is being said, but also in understanding the person who is saying it. Listening is a dual process. I listen and you listen, we learn about each other, we grow in understanding and we grow closer either to each other or a needed resolution. Listening includes inquiry, patience, the ability to avoid seeking immediate resolution, and the willingness to hang in uncertainty for as long as it takes.

Asking

Asking requires curiosity in a different flavor of interest than mentioned above. This interest incluzdes emotional investment, willingness to sacrifice time and ego and the vulnerability involved in not knowing. After asking in this manner, our listening is greatly enhanced, as is our ability to understand.

Listening Again

When listening again, we open ourselves and the other person to greater understanding. Listening again does not have to include repetition—but it can if it is needed. But the goal of listening again has to do with mutual interest, caring and commitment to have the discussion bring us closer—it represents our assurance to our partner that we are not only looking to win or be heard/understood; that our goal is to make space for their point of view.

Agreeing and resolution are then consequences of the dance as opposed to the goal we are trying to reach when "dancing".

Sharing

If we have in fact, listened, asked and listened again (LALA) in the way described above, we are in a position to Share. A point worth observing is that after LALA, "Sharing" is a true contribution. Because we have taken the time to understand and connect, our sharing can be made in a non-confrontational manner, even in cases where the content is not agreement or resolution. Consider that this kind of sharing is born from an intention to connect and understand instead of make wrong or prove right. People involved in a LALAS conversational dance are clear that learning and growing is of greater worth than anything else.

You may be worrying that following the LALAS steps would be time-consuming. As a matter of fact, any new skill requires time to learn and implement. But LALAS gives way to mutual trust and understanding, which often results in the ability to have shorthand discussions.

A NOTE: If communication is the fastest route
to improve, heal, restore, maintain and nurture
relationships, then an insistence on winning, losing,
putting people down, confrontation, etc. must all be
considered communicational missteps.

Being self-aware of the intention behind each
comment and question will help you assess
how you are contributing to the dance.

Pausing as a Tool

We have been trained to expect instant gratification and resist—even resent—the need to wait. But developing a practice of pausing, particularly when the pause is opening a space for us to wait for ourselves, can provide an amazing resource for confident and purposeful behavior.

Pausing grants equal opportunity to everyone in a conversation to momentarily stop the interaction, examine their personal contribution to the dynamic, and reboot their approach. Successful pausing must include:

A request for a pause from either person in the conversation. We can ask for a pause anytime a conversation is reaching a point when we:

- Notice we are not listening
- Feel the need to repeatedly interrupt
- Feel overwhelmed by emotions we cannot name
- Have an intent to win
- Are clear that we can not collaborate
- Lack interest in the other's position

When a request for a pause is made, the conversation will be temporarily suspended with the support of all parties. This support is given without resentment and is for the benefit of all involved.

A clear amount of time the pause will take: this means that all parties agree to the amount of time the pause will take and will honor that agreement.

These steps ensure that the pausing has a positive impact, enhances trust and serves to support all involved.

Values Tool

Values play an important role in how we interact with people in our lives. Apart from ourselves, no one is affected deeper by our values than those closest to us, such as our immediate family. Identifying our primary values can afford us a view into ourselves that is otherwise difficult to see.

Read through the following words. As you read, place a check mark (✓) next to the words that pull at your attention or seem more important. Go back to the list and only look at the check-marked words. Circle those that you recognize as personal traits. Go back to the list and only look at the circled words. Which ones are non-negotiable for you? You must reduce your list to 5 words. In most cases, these are the values that rule the way you see and interact with the world.

Acceptance	Challenge	Courage	Energy
Accomplishment	Charity	Courtesy	Enjoyment
Accountability	Cleanliness	Creation	Enthusiasm
Accuracy	Clear	Creativity	Equality
Achievement	Clever	Credibility	Ethical
Adaptability	Comfort	Curiosity	Excellence
Alertness	Commitment	Decisive	Experience
Altruism	Common sense	Decisiveness	Giving
Ambition	Communication	Dedication	Exploration
Amusement	Community	Dependability	Expressive
Assertiveness	Compassion	Determination	Fairness
Attentive	Competence	Development	Family
Awareness	Concentration	Devotion	Famous
Balance	Confidence	Dignity	Fearless
Boldness	Connection	Discipline	Feelings
Bravery	Consciousness	Discovery	Ferocious
Brilliance	Consistency	Drive	Fidelity
Calm	Contentment	Effectiveness	Focus
Candor	Contribution	Efficiency	Foresight
Capable	Control	Empathy	Fortitude
Careful	Conviction	Empower	Freedom
Certainty	Cooperation	Endurance	Friendship

Fun	Leadership	Recreation	Support
Generosity	Learning	Reflective	Surprise
Genius	Liberty	Respect	Sustainability
Goodness	Logic	Responsibility	Talent
Grace	Love	Restraint	Teamwork
Gratitude	Loyalty	Results-oriented	Temperance
Greatness	Mastery	Reverence	Thankful
Growth	Maturity	Rigor	Thorough
Happiness	Meaning	Risk	Thoughtful
Hard work	Moderation	Satisfaction	Timeliness
Harmony	Motivation	Security	Tolerance
Health	Openness	Self-reliance	Toughness
Honesty	Optimism	Selfless	Traditional
Honor	Order	Sensitivity	Tranquility
Hope	Organization	Serenity	Transparency
Humility	Originality	Service	Trust
Imagination	Passion	Sharing	Trustworthy
Improvement	Patience	Significance	Truth
Independence	Peace	Silence	Understanding
Individuality	Performance	Simplicity	Uniqueness
Innovation	Persistence	Sincerity	Unity
Inquisitive	Playfulness	Skill	Valor
Insightful	Poise	Skillfulness	Victory
Inspiring	Potential	Smart	Vigor
Integrity	Power	Solitude	Vision
Intelligence	Present	Spirit	Vitality
Intensity	Productivity	Spirituality	Wealth
Intuitive	Professionalism	Spontaneous	Welcoming
Irreverent	Prosperity	Stability	Winning
Joy	Purpose	Status	Wisdom
Justice	Quality	Stewardship	Wonder
Kindness	Realistic	Strength	
Knowledge	Reason	Structure	
Lawful	Recognition	Success	

Resources

There have been many resources discussed throughout the book. Continuing to read, discuss and learn will help you and your intimate partner grow in your relationship. Communication is the key and these resources will continue to expand your ability to nurture knowledge in your relationship.

www.thehijackedbrainbook.com

Love Languages, Gary Chapman

You can heal your life, Louise Hay

Conversational Intelligence, Judith Glazer

How to hug a porcupine, John Lewis Lund

The Gifts of Imperfection, Brené Brown

What Makes Love Last? John Gottman

www.5lovelanguages.com

www.nytimes.com/interactive/projects/modern-love/36-questions/

TED Talks

Kelly McGonigal: How to make stress your friend
www.ted.com/talks/kelly_mcgonigal_how_to_make_stress_your_friend

Esther Perel: Rethinking infidelity
www.ted.com/talks/esther_perel_rethinking_infidelity_a_talk_for_anyone_who_has_ever_loved

Brené Brown: The power of vulnerability
https://www.ted.com/talks/brene_brown_on_vulnerability

chapter twelve

Final Thoughts

We hope that this has been an amazing journey for you through what can be a very difficult topic for couples to discuss. Our expectations were designed to help you see that:

- You are not alone in your experiences.
- Everyone is impacted in some way by a Hijacked Brain.
- There are tools and resources that can help you and your intimate partner.
- There are biological causes for both women and men regarding their individual reactions to a Hijacked Brain.

- The ability to communicate is vital to any relationship, but you must be able to share your thoughts, feelings, desires, and needs in your intimate relationship without fear of rejection and with the hope of love and understanding.

The growth that you have learned is now your knowledge to share with others. Imagine the possibility of sharing this hope with friends, family, colleagues, and your own children to help all see that the experience is normal but that you can control how you respond.

Also, do not end your reading with the thought that your learning is complete. You may find yourself needing to read certain sections again. The tools are designed for you to do as often as needed. Continue to read and review the resources listed previously; and frequently review the website at *www.fireintheweeds.com* for additional readings, posts, and resources, including coaches and counselors located near you.

A Special Message For Therapists

To the Therapists and Relationships Coaches

We respectfully reach out to you, the professionals that carry the responsibility to assisting couples, and ask that you come into this community of dedicated professionals. Our task is large and of great importance. Individuals are losing themselves and each other to an unspoken yet treatable problem.

Take stock of your own awareness on this topic; maybe you already ask the right questions and have noticed patterns. But have you noticed the difficulty level to bring this issue up to a couple? Have you noticed the actual and potential reaction in your clients when you mention a relationship between behavioral changes when a brain is hijacked?

The following pages bring up some points to keep in mind as you traverse these murky waters. We rely on your acceptance of our respect for your skills and experience, hoping that our input serves as encouragement to tackle this issues head on and help individuals and couples see their part in the dynamic in their lives.

Having a therapeutic mindset, one that insists that individuals are already equipped to resolve their concerns, makes us more curious, which ignites more questions which keep the client in conversation. Insight is a result of the process of outward, witnessed and challenged introspection. The client speaks, we witness and challenge, and they arrive at hidden information that illuminates behavior and choice.

Where to Begin

Diagnosing seems to be an important part of what we do as therapists, but when it comes to couples, there is nothing in the DSM-5 to assist us. Conventional couples' treatment has us looking at the individuals and their possible emotional and psychological shortcomings in order to understand where their issues are coming from. Often, diagnosing individually requires that we look for their deficiencies.

We encourage a holistic approach—one that looks at dynamics, the couple's history, individual and together beliefs, honesty level in the relationship, and ability of the individuals to self-acknowledge. In other words, a holistic approach requires that we look at the couple as one entity with the individuals as contributing parts—all relevant, all important and indicative of the issues at hand and the already-available solutions.

We suggest that a couple's intake can span over 3-6 sessions as follows:

Session 1-3: Couples decompress by actively rehearsing the "problems" they are facing. During these sessions, insight is difficult to impart or achieve. You are tasked with making them aware that during these sessions your goal is primarily to listen, learn, and assign them needed research (homework) that will help you do your job. Warning them ahead of time will serve to lower their expectation for a quick fix and get greater buy-in for attendance to early sessions.

Sessions 2-5: Questions are the name of the game at this point. See how their answers match or mismatch. Introspective questions make them become more vulnerable to the therapist and to each other, making these sessions the basis for the therapeutic goal. What to ask? Anything that will help you become clearer about:
- What has been said
- What they are presenting as an issue or as their goals
- Any conflicting stories, timelines, wishes, etc.
- Learn about their beliefs on relationships
- Their cultural expectations
- Can they report on triggers, times of greater difficulty, etc.
- What other types of help have they sought—when, why, did it work
- Assess their care level, anger level, commitment level, honesty capacity
- Pay attention to the weaknesses but identify what works
  - Do they recognize what works
  - Can they capitalize on their strengths
- Are they able to partner at any level

During this thorough investigation, assign tasks that will illuminate information they have taken for granted but can be used in therapy to reach their goals.

Sessions 3-6: Through the questioning already completed, some degree of insight should have been gained by the individuals. Getting them to verbalize this clearly is a must, as it will be an indication of their ability to self-observe and integrate. Therapeutic goals are developed during this phase, including the therapist's boundaries, rules, and expectations. Here are some examples:

- Individuals must understand that the information provided is taken as factual and will be used to benefit the couple and reach goals
- Individual "secrets" are perceived as harmful to the therapy and to the relationship
- The therapist can and will serve as a mediator to confront hard truths and realities, but is not responsible for misinformation, holdbacks, or deceit by the clients
- Should the therapist determine that "things don't add up", that will be clearly stated and the clients are held as responsible to make sense of the information on the table
- The therapist is not to take part in collusion with either party and is free to terminate treatment should this be an expectation by either party
- The therapist will maintain a clear measure of the commitment of the couple and may recommend alternate modalities (individual, group, psychiatric/medicine, etc) as deemed needed to achieve goals
- The therapist should and will terminate treatment if couple's behavior evidences less interest than that of the therapist
- Any other boundaries, rules, or expectations deemed needed by the professional

By way of modeling, the therapist will hold all expectations as "conversation topics" which the client(s) can bring up for discussion as needed. This modeling will serve to show the couples that there are no absolutes and negotiation, accommodation, and re-establishing agreements is always possible.

Begin Early

Setting up a partnership with the couples we work with is imperative. For this reason, it is imperative that the individuals are aware that:

- Research is expected. Our efforts to "get to the bottom of things" will be futile unless they contribute to the needed research in full. Research is completed by the couple via assignments completed between sessions
- Partnership only happens when honesty is absolute. It is a reasonable expectation that the therapist will assist in gaining communication skills and coping mechanisms to deal with difficult realities. However, the therapist should not work with individuals unwilling to face and communicate their realities.
- Seek to identify how well they can partner and in what areas they do that well. Encourage the nurturing of partnership in areas already present and look for ways to help partnership emerge in new ones.

Resources ONLY for therapists

Please visit our website for tools, training, supervision opportunities and new articles and resources that will further your work.

We are only an email away!

Definitions

When speaking about the issues that are being covered in this book, it is important to make sure we are talking about the same things. You've seen it before when you say something, meaning one thing, yet the listener interprets what you said differently. There are many reasons for this, including factors that we cover throughout, like emotional intelligence and mindfulness. The hope in this chapter is to get us all on the same page.

As you read the definitions of key terms below, realize that this is the definition we use when you see throughout the additional material. This will help you realize our intent, but also as you discuss with your intimate partner there should be less confusion.

Key Terms Defined

Intimate Relationships—formal construct (marriage, couplehood, committed partnerships, etc.) where individuals are working to live and work together toward common goals and include exclusivity, sexual interest, and interactions

Hijacked Brain—period of time (days) when an individual feels carried away by emotions and unable to feel in control of reactions and thoughts

Self-Awareness—being aware of your own behaviors, emotions and characteristics

Emotional Intelligence—possessing the ability to manage not only your own emotions but the emotions of others by identifying, applying, and regulating emotions

Codependent—type of relationship that is often one-sided and can be emotionally/abusive destructive; these relationships are unhappy and unhealthy, but is very hard for the individual to leave

Depression—there are many signs/symptoms of depression, but this definition includes feelings of sadness, low energy, and hopelessness that impact your ability to function

Empathy—the ability to understand or identify with your intimate partner's emotions or situation

Commitment—the act of being devoted to your intimate partner emotionally, physically, and spiritually

Intimate Compassion Fatigue—the emotional strain within a relationship when behaviors, actions, and communication are inconsistent with the rest of the relationship. Intimate compassion fatigue occurs over the course of time with continued exposure to the inconsistencies without the experience changing for the positive.

Mindfulness—being aware of your and your intimate partner's experiences, emotions, and behaviors without being judgmental; it is an act of curiosity to understand

Effective communication—the open and honest interchange of ideas with a foundation in curiosity and relationship bound interest

Effective Intimate Relationships—space where all involved are fully self-expressed and where that expression is revered and encouraged, and vulnerability is rewarded with equal openness and honesty

Listening—act of being present and non-judgmentally paying attention to what is being said

Double-Clicking—practice of refusing to assume we know what our intimate partner means and instead invites a deeper communication regarding their thoughts and feelings

Emotional Triggers—these are the words or behaviors that can cause either a positive or negative reaction to you or your intimate partner

Cortisol—the hormone produced by the adrenal cortex that becomes elevated in response to physical or psychological stress; activates protective behavior

Oxytocin—the hormone produced by the pituitary gland that stimulates feelings of connection and closeness; it is released during moments of trust and promotes connectivity

Rigid Partner—there are many characteristics of someone who is rigid, but this definition includes those intimate partners who have a very difficult time with change, trying new things, or being curious

There may be other terms or keywords that you find as you read that are not defined here. If you believe there can be more than one way to interpret or define a term, please be sure to discuss with your intimate partner and come to an agreement on what you both believe the word or phrase means. When you are both on the same page and communicating with the same language, you will be amazed at the reduction in stress and the increase in clarity that effective communication can bring to your relationship!

The Authors

About Nathalie

My name is Nathalie Concepcion. This is the way we introduce each other in person so it makes sense to start with that in writing. I can't wait for the day when books are interactive and you can introduce yourself to me. I would want to know: what is happening in your life? What made you pick up this book? What are you hoping to find? Bob and I wrote this for you and hope that the answers to your questions are easy to find in these pages and in the insight you gain as you read.

As you will be spending time reading our words we thought you'd want to know a bit about us. So, here you go:

In my personal life I am a self-admitted Pollyanna. I am practical in most of my views, yet open to and curious of how other people interact with life and the circumstances it presents. While it cannot be said that I've had a hard life, it is true that I have experienced tough times.

I grew up in the Dominican Republic, in what today would be considered a mid-income life style. There, I experienced natural disasters that changed life in a matter of hours; saw my parents experience financial hardships; left all I knew to involuntarily follow my parents to the United States at the age of 15; experienced the terrifying suspense of having a baby born sick and not knowing if she would make it; and I have been hurt by people I loved and trusted and I have lost treasured relationships. I have known loneliness and emotional desperation—even depression. But amidst those historical facts there have been incredible experiences like falling in love, reaching desired goals, getting married and having babies who today, even as the adults they have become, fill my life with pride and joy.

Now joy has been a trademark of mine from age zero. Those closest to me would agree that even in the worst of times I found a silver lining, a lesson to be learned, or a way to strengthen faith. Having said that, and while in the scope of personal information, faith is a topic worth exploring. From age 15 to age 48 I was devotedly religious. Today I identify as deeply spiritual but not committed to any one institution. This position is held as of value to me and never imposed on anyone regardless of the type of relationship we share. My spiritual views and commitment are personal and center on a connection to something bigger than myself.

Also in the realm of personal information, it seems necessary to state that I am divorced. That particular life experience led me to commit to my professional goals with passion. I aim to meaningfully contribute to a world where individuals come in and out of intimate relationships whole, capable, and complete: *Whole* as in nothing missing in themselves; *Capable* as in able to manage the inevitable ups and downs of life, able to incorporate what is needed to live a joyful life; and *Complete* as in not requiring more, finding satisfaction with life as it is.

Note that *Complete* gives way to effort to achieve out of determination, instead of need or lack. I am clear, personally and professionally, that for this to come to pass, individuals must shift from the consensus that being coupled is a requirement to life fulfillment. I can subscribe to the idea that couple-hood is desirable but refuse the notion that it is required for happiness and fulfillment.

My professional life has experienced a number of incarnations as I adapted to family needs and responsibilities. As time allowed, I completed a Masters in Social Work, continuous postgraduate training towards support of earned clinical license, and a Masters in Business with a Concentration in Organizational Behavior, and an Executive Coach certificate. I have been in private practice with a focus on couples treatment since 1999 and have treated hundreds of couples. Some have remained married and some parted ways, but all individuals gained insights into their participation and contribution to the fate of their relationship.

My extensive training, coupled with personal sensibilities, afford me multiple views of any situation and an ability to communicate those observations clearly, forging workability and partnership for anyone interested in my assistance to grow and develop.

I met Bob McCullough during an event where we were representing our mutual employer; to say that he is a genuinely kind person and a consummate professional is a description that falls short. In a brief span of time Bob went from stranger to respected colleague and friend. Our professional responsibilities made it possible for us to partner up to complete multiple assignments, share clinical observations, and resolve to write this book together. Bob has had a lasting impact in my life. He has added confirmation to my long-held understanding that men and women can work closely together, call each other friends—even confidants—without ever crossing lines that would compromise valued commitments.

I think I was always going to write a book. One thing is certain, this book could not have been written without my colleague and friend Bob McCullough.

For more information, please visit the book's website:

www.thehijackedbrainbook.com

or my personal website:

www.nathalieconcepcion.com.

About Bob

This is a book about relationships. While primarily you will see the personal stories, examples, and focus will be on intimate relationships, I believe there is going to be helpful information as well as tools that you can use across any and all relationships you experience. However, before you can grow a relationship you have to know a little about the person. That is the goal of this section.

As Nathalie so accurately set forth, we would really enjoy getting to know each of you. To have that opportunity to hear your stories and personal experiences would grow us as clinicians and people, but also help add life to what you will be reading in the pages to come. Until that technology is developed or we are able to meet, what I can do is share a bit about me.

Professionally, I have held a number of different roles within the behavioral health field. My story would look familiar to many counselors: community work, inpatient setting, outpatient, case manager, residential, private practice, and several leadership roles in managed care and digital behavioral health. However, there are a few key roles that have really helped guide my contribution on this project.

Private practice working with kids/families: For several years I provided counseling to children who were involved in foster care and their families. You can learn a lot about the impact of trust, hope, and bonding working with kids in the system and the importance that "just being there" can have on a relationship.

Pre-marital/marital counseling: For years I have assisted churches with pre-marital counseling. To see young couples with fresh love filled with anticipation is always a blessing. And while there is never a desire to squash that anticipation, there does need to be the walk with them regarding how they will grow and stay in love when it comes to household chores, grocery shopping, raising children, and managing a budget. Those are not always seen as the "fun" parts of marriage, but instead of dreading them, it is an honor to show couples how you can grow together in all marital activities you do.

Similarly, counseling couples who have struggles in their marriage is where a large portion of my experience and content come. These couples have had the full range of issues including affairs, abuse, separation, and seeing counseling as the absolute last stage before divorce. There are always multiple reasons why couples struggle, yet so often I hear "she did this" or "if he would just change" when blaming is never going to help. It takes two to fight but also takes two to love, and helping couples who are truly interested in saving their marriage can be some of the most rewarding work of which I can be a part.

Crisis response: I have had the opportunity to be part of some of the largest crises that have occurred in recent memory, including the terrorist attacks of September 11, 2001, Hurricane Katrina, nightclub shootings, workplace terror, and other community and natural disasters. I've learned a few valuable lessons along the way. First, the true heroes are first responders and we should thank them every chance we get for the way they respond when crisis occurs. Second, everyone is impacted by a crisis. For many, their emotional reactions are short-term and their resiliency will kick in to return to "normal" functioning. But for others, the crisis may be the trigger that sets them into deep emotional turmoil. The impact that a crisis can have on a person and, in turn, their relationships became a focus for me to help them realize that they do not have to experience the crisis alone and that caring relationships will help them recover.

Personally, let me try to share some of the info about myself from questions that I would be asking you if we were having lunch. The first question would be about your current relationship. For me, it's a fun story to tell: I married my high school sweetheart, which means we literally have grown up together. We went to different colleges—but in the same city—and married right after college graduation. We experienced being poor college students, but we had love and hope (which gets you through a great deal more than money ever will).

The next question would be about your family and the impact they have on you. I would share with you that besides my wife I currently have three adult children: two boys and a girl who are all three different, yet similar. Our hope in having kids was that they would be close enough in age to grow up together and, therefore, be close as adults. Looks like that has happened, because even though they live in separate places they remain close, and as parents that brings us great joy. What also helps, especially with this project, is that all three of my children are in that "adulting" stage of dating and making future life plans. It is interesting to get those questions about life, and even more encouraging that they still want to hear what we have to say... sometimes.

Our next topic of conversation might be around who the relationships or people were that taught you how to be an intimate partner or spouse. My share is that I grew up with my mom, dad, and two younger brothers. We grew up in a semi-rural area but days were filled playing some type of sport and thinking of ways to torment my brothers (there is something to be said about birth order, especially when you are the oldest). I would also let you know that—in full disclosure—my parents had a marriage full of struggles that ended in divorce after 25 years of being married. My wife's parents (whom I've known since age 16) have also been influential, especially at this point. My mom-in-law has been struggling with serious health issues for several years and my dad-in-law has been remarkable in how he has stepped up to provide a role I'm sure he never expected, yet every day he shows tremendous love, support, and care.

Considering this is a relationship book, one of the topics we might cover over this very long lunch is to hear some of the stories that have defined your relationship/marriage. Remember, my wife and I have grown up together, so we have many stories to tell. The stories would include the tremendous fun and butterflies of dating, getting married, and the birth of children. They would also include the struggles of finances, work, managing a home and raising [those] children, the joy and stress of building a new home, and several moves in between. I could talk about the importance of staying connected to your partner as the kids get older and start to leave the home, and the transition to being "empty nesters." (Fun note: it really can be emotionally difficult yet very exciting for the next chapter in your life as well.)

As we continue to get to know one another, there would be so many questions that would continue to come up. But as we start to wrap up the lunch, I would want to know what is important to you, essentially what drives you. For me it starts with faith. As far as relationships go, the one I have with God defines who I am and strive to be. While faith can be a whole separate lunch topic, much of what drives me comes from this relationship. I have a desire to always show joy, kindness, goodness, and respect to all, whether or not they show it back. I want to be genuine and straightforward yet do so with compassion and tact. I want to know you and others so that we can learn, grow, and help each other. In full disclosure, I don't know everything, and while I attempt to be all the above, I struggle and fail often. Fortunately, life gives plenty of chances to do right and learn from previous experiences.

As our lunch has ended and we are saying goodbye, I would be encouraging about what you are about to embark and learn from me and Nathalie. She has introduced herself and provided a bit of our background, but I can't say enough about how truly blessed I am to call her friend. She has a knowledge, experience, and a way of communicating that I know you will find helpful and desiring for more. So stay open, take notes, be honest regarding yourself and relationships, and lets start a journey together.

www.ingramcontent.com/pod-product-compliance
Lightning Source LLC
Chambersburg PA
CBHW072134020426
42334CB00018B/1795